TUNED IN

The Power of Pressing Pause and Listening

TUNED IN

The Power of Pressing Pause and Listening

ART AND LARAINE BENNETT

Our Sunday Visitor

www.osv.com
Our Sunday Visitor Publishing Division
Our Sunday Visitor, Inc.
Huntington, Indiana 46750

ABOUT THE AUTHORS

ART BENNETT is currently the president and chief executive officer (CEO) of Catholic Charities in the Diocese of Arlington, Virginia. He was also the co-founder and director of the Alpha Omega Clinics in Maryland and Virginia (2002–2010). He has more than thirty years' experience in the mental health field and is a frequent speaker on marriage and family issues.

LARAINE BENNETT has a master's degree in philosophy and is the communications manager for the National Council of Catholic Women.

Together, the Bennetts have co-authored three popular books on temperament (*The Temperament God Gave You*, *The Temperament God Gave Your Spouse*, and the *Temperament God Gave Your Kids*) in addition to their book *The Emotions God Gave You*. Laraine wrote *A Year of Grace: 365 Reflections for Caregivers*.

Art and Laraine have been married for forty years.

To Dylan, Micah, and Baby Bennett

CONTENTS

ACKNOWLEDGMENTS

We are grateful to Pope Francis, who challenges us to bring the good news of God's mercy beyond our comfort zone, especially to the margins, and to view our Church as a "field hospital." His emphasis on encounter, listening, and accompaniment inspires us continually. In the words of Saint Catherine of Siena, he is our own "sweet Christ on earth."

We are grateful to Bert Ghezzi for his friendship and editorial leadership; we wish him happy retirement! And we gratefully acknowledge Mary Beth Baker's editorial guidance and assistance.

We are especially grateful to our family, whose love fills our hearts with happiness and laughter, giving us a glimpse of that heavenly wedding feast we one day hope to enjoy.

***

Unless otherwise noted, Scripture citations are from the *Revised Standard Version of the Bible — Second Catholic Edition* (Ignatius Edition), copyright © 1965, 1966, 2006 National Council of the Churches of Christ in the United States of America. Used by permission. All rights reserved. Where noted, other Scripture citations are from the *New American Bible, revised edition* copyright © 2010, 1991, 1986, 1970 Confraternity of Christian Doctrine, Washington, D.C., and are used

CHAPTER 1

Listening:
The Most Important Thing

We were spending a leisurely evening at a dinner party hosted by acquaintances. As we engaged in spirited conversation with a couple whom we had just met, both of us had the same negative reaction. Whenever we would bring up a potential topic for discussion or put forward a unique fact about ourselves — for example, the fact that we once lived in Germany for more than four years with small children — they would give a perfunctory nod, and then they immediately launched into a passionate monologue about how they, too, had had a similar experience: "Once, we took a cruise down the Rhine…." It was as though they could barely wait for us to finish our sentence before they jumped in with an "I'll see your Germany, and I will raise you our Rhineland cruise!"

By the end of the evening, we were exhausted and grumpy. We grumbled all the way home about how we felt one-upped by the couple. "They were prideful, disrespectful, and boorish," we harrumphed.

But God has a way of gently helping us face our own sinfulness, without actually rubbing our noses in it.

Not long after, we hosted our own dinner party. We were magnanimous and gregarious, holding forth on myriad subjects. We told personal stories and embellished upon the shyly proffered attempts at conversation by some of the younger guests. At one point, Laraine caught herself cutting off a comment to rush in with her own, more interesting story. Suddenly, as though the Holy Spirit shined a laser-beam spotlight on the moment, she realized she was exhibiting the very same behavior she (and Art) had recently so deeply resented. Both of us had thought we were being good hosts, moving the conversation forward and bonding through stories with our guests. Alas, we were barely listening at all.

Why listen, anyway? Is it just a matter of etiquette, an Emily Post rule for social interaction? Do we listen to be polite, pausing for a discreet moment while waiting for our turn to speak? Is it, perhaps, simply the first step in acquiring information or a strategic move on the part of a skilled politician or apologist? Is it an effort to learn about people and motivate them?

In fact, it is much more than that: it is the *most important* thing. As Pope Emeritus Benedict XVI said, "The most important thing for everyone is to listen: to listen to each other, and for everyone to listen to what the Lord wants to say to us."[1] Pope Francis reminds us, "Listening is more than hearing. It's a mutual listening in which each one has something to learn."[2]

A Scarce Commodity

I am standing at the counter in front of my laptop, scrolling through Facebook posts from friends and just-barely-acquaintances, some of whom I've never met in person. I am skipping past the "And you will never guess what happened when she did THIS" teasers and the angry political diatribes, drooling over recipe videos, and rolling my eyes over yet another alleged Pope Francis gaffe. Then I gradually become aware of an insistent whine, a plaintive, soft rumble. I drag my eyes away from my laptop to see my little poodle, Ginger, woefully gazing at me with large brown eyes and wet nose. She needs to go out.

I wonder: How many times have I missed something important, something real — or worse, some*one* real — right here in the room while I zoned out, hypnotized by Facebook? How many times have I neglected morning prayer because of the siren call of the Internet?

Listening is becoming a scarce commodity in our fast-paced, efficiency-minded, technologically driven society. Because we communicate so quickly these days, the lag time between query and response has diminished, sometimes to the point of missing important information or even displaying rudeness.

One writer has likened social media to a mugger; it demands your attention and holds you hostage until you respond. But these responses are not always thoughtful, nor do they require true listening. Rather than fostering communication, they sometimes inhibit it and promote angry stalemates, lines drawn in the sand. In 2015, when the terror attacks in Paris unfolded on November 13, and a few weeks later (on December 2) the tragedy in San Bernardino, our Facebook feeds exploded with angry epithets hurled back and forth in virtual space. And, as a nation, we saw this all too clearly throughout the 2016 election season.

Today, as we are bombarded by noise and our attention is constantly demanded by social media, we have become accustomed to sound bites that glance along the surface of our intellects like pebbles skimming across water. The very texture of our lives has become imbued with the hectic quality of technology, with efficiency and productivity becoming our primary goal while human beings are seen as mere resources.

Things that take time — reading a Dickens novel, baking a pie from scratch, listening to an opera, or sitting at the bedside of someone in the nursing home — these activities get pushed to the back burner.

Drowning in Communication

We have never had more information available at our fingertips — all the world's knowledge instantly accessible via Google — yet we have never been more impersonal, more isolated. Studies have shown that with increased online activity comes increased depression, loneliness, and alienation; more people are feeling isolated and lonely, even while entertaining hundreds of "friends" in the digital world. And men and women addicted to pornography find themselves unable to maintain true intimate relationships with real people. In a tragic irony, in 2014, a college track star posted happy photos on social media minutes before committing suicide. Being surrounded by digital forms of communication can isolate rather than draw us together.

Pope Benedict XVI identified a serious issue facing contemporary society, one which Pope Francis continues to focus on: "The great communication ... that we have today can lead, on the one hand, to complete depersonalization. Then one is just swimming in a sea of communication and no longer encounters persons at all."[3]

A single friend of mine recently wrote a series of lovely blog posts on the subject of creating a beautiful Catholic home. She prefaced these posts by carefully explaining that she was not trying to say that women must have a perfectly tidy home at all times, lest they be considered spiritual and moral slackers. She was not suggesting that Catholic moms must be Martha Stewarts. Nonetheless, she found herself facing a whirlwind of angry, tearful comments from insulted mothers. They asked how she dared even discuss the concept of a Catholic home when she didn't have children. They assumed the worst: the author was trying to shame those mothers with messy homes filled with toddlers and babies and animals — how dare she! The impersonal, instantaneous nature of the blogosphere creates an environment in which misunderstanding and distrust abound.

TUNED IN: The Power of Pressing Pause and Listening

Are we drowning in communication? Is the constant bombardment made possible by our ubiquitous technology, a surround sound of information, isolating and dividing us?

In January 2017, we took public transportation into our nation's capital for the annual March for Life. We noticed how many people were shutting *out* their environment — including people around them — by having earbuds plugged into their ears. They were not attending to the real world — or people — around them, too busy listening to their own music. But were they listening? Or were they only "hearing" their own music?

We should pause here to make a distinction, one that Pope Francis alluded to when he said that "listening is more than hearing." We can hear something without *attending to it*, without an intentionality of purpose.

With the rise of technology and the ease with which we can have the entire world available to us at a single keystroke, with the demands on our already fragmented attention spans, and with the fact that people are feeling more and more isolated, we need to attend purposefully to *persons. This purposeful attention is listening.* Listening involves attention. It requires an active focus and a desire to *be with*, to encounter, another. Listening is not isolated and solitary, like plugging in our earbuds, nor is it a passive activity; it is intensely interpersonal and active. Listening is an intentional activity.

Perhaps it is misleading to begin this section by saying we are "drowning in communication." It might be more accurate to say we are drowning in sound bites, in words designed to sell us a product, in stimulation of the senses, in media, in technology. This sort of communication is, in reality, a form of grasping and taking, a relationship to things and a using of people as things. What we are missing is a simple being with, a reverence in the presence of the other.

The true meaning of communication is *communion with, sharing, a give-and-take process with another person* — not merely sharing information but drawing closer to one another through this sharing. But we are getting ahead of ourselves. The difference between hearing and listening, and the true purpose of communication, will become more apparent as we read on.

One Simple Thing

Wouldn't it be amazing if there was one small thing you could do each day that could transform all your relationships and make them 100 percent better? What if there was one simple thing that, if everyone did it, would result in world peace?

There is. It's called listening.

Laraine visits a nursing home on First Fridays to bring Holy Communion to the elderly and sick. One gentleman is only in his fifties, but he is confined to bed due to a degenerative disease. He rarely speaks and when he does, it is a whisper. But the last time she visited him, he actually spoke out loud! Laraine was astonished and exclaimed, "I'm so happy to hear your voice!" His face lit up at the same time as he asked, bewildered, "But why?"

And that's a good question. Why do we need to hear his voice? Why do we listen so carefully when he whispers? We have seen the residents of the nursing home who have slipped away into silence, their fragile bodies turned toward the wall, their eyes glazed over in resignation. We don't want him to slip away into an uncommunicative silence. We want him to know that we care about him. And we want to hear about him, and who he is. He enriches our lives.

The Art of Listening

In today's environment, it is all the more necessary, then, to foster the *virtue* of listening — or better, the *art* of listening.

Listening is an art, not a skill. Pope Benedict wrote:

> To listen means to know and to acknowledge another and to allow him to step into the realm of one's own "I".... Thus, after the act of listening, I am another man, my own being is enriched and deepened because it is united with the being of the other....[4]

Like any art or virtue, it can be learned and practiced. And why? So that we can grow closer to our loved ones and closer to God.

As Pope Francis says,

> Good communication helps us to grow closer, to know one another better, and ultimately, to grow in

unity. The walls which divide us can be broken down only if we are prepared to listen and learn from one another. We need to resolve our differences through forms of dialogue which help us grow in understanding and mutual respect. A culture of encounter demands that we be ready not only to give, but also to receive.[5]

As a marriage and family therapist (Art), and as speakers and authors of several Catholic practical books for engaged couples, spouses, and parents (Art and Laraine), we believe that there is a need to address this simplest — yet foundational — aspect of all human relationships.

The first step in discipleship is listening. Jesus' disciples heard his call. There must have been a cacophony of voices all around: the crowds clamoring for a miracle, the Pharisees denouncing and challenging him, the moaning of the sick and the wailing of the possessed. Yet there was the quiet, authoritative voice of Jesus saying, "Follow me."

This book is about listening:

- Listening to God, listening to others.
- Listening to your heart, your body, wisdom, criticism.
- Listening to the silence.

And it's about:

- Practical ways we can improve our listening skills.

- Real-life situations where we forgot to listen and things quickly went south.
- Real-life situations where we did, by the grace of God, listen.

We need to listen to one another, to God, and to the Church in order to truly walk with our fellow travelers. This notion of accompaniment is particularly significant for Pope Francis. He is calling for a genuine culture of encountering people. He is showing us how to truly "evangelize" — our primary vocation as Christians — to love and to bring Christ's love to all our brothers and sisters. To be loving, we must listen. Pope Francis writes in *Evangelii Gaudium* that

> The Church will have to initiate everyone — priests, religious and laity — into this "art of accompaniment" which teaches us to remove our sandals before the sacred ground of the other (cf. Ex 3:5). The pace of this accompaniment must be steady and reassuring, reflecting our closeness and our compassionate gaze which also heals, liberates and encourages growth in the Christian life.[6]

In a world ever more strident, ever more politicized, we need to find spaces where we can walk gently with one another so that our common hopes and dreams can be glimpsed. And in that healing moment of understanding, we can be brought together, just as Christ longed for us to be.

In the chapters that follow, we will present real-life situations where listening is vital for body, mind, and soul — where sometimes we fail to listen and other times we succeed. Each chapter will include a short scriptural reflection or quote from the saints as well as a practical listening skill or virtue that readers can practice.

— PRACTICAL APPLICATION —

Being Silent

Many times we are afraid to be empathic because we think empathy means we "agree with" what the other person is saying. Before we can even decide whether or not we agree, we must first understand. But understanding and being empathic is not simply a matter of hearing and parroting back, "I hear you saying you are feeling lonely" and then jumping to a swift solution to the problem. Before we work on being fully present, attentive, and empathic, we are going to need to learn how *not* to react. We are going to have to practice *being silent*.

This may be an easier assignment for introverts than for extraverts. Extraverts always find it easy to carry —and sometimes dominate — the conversation and are often accused of failing to listen. But introverts have their own foibles. A naturally shy person may be intimidated by the prospect of carrying a conversation, and may find himself monologuing or inappropriately latching onto one word that was said and effectively derailing the conversation. Most often, however, we have difficulty being silent because we disagree with what the other person is saying. We think we must immediately respond and nip the discussion in the bud. We think that listening to them, hearing them out, is equivalent to agreeing with them.

Now you have to be ready for this. It won't be easy. But the payoff, down the road, is remarkable. Ready? Okay.

1. **Press the pause button.** This week, let's practice pressing the pause button, as Art likes to say. Make a decision that during one conversation or one meeting today, you will be silent, just listening to a person when you would typically respond. It might be your spouse, a child, a co-worker, a neighbor. Just pick someone and radically listen. Not thinking in your mind all the responses you will make as soon as the person takes a breath. Not thinking about the Yankees, not wishing you were on the beach, not coming up with responses in your head, but dying to yourself and being fully present to the other person. Take a moment to find peace within yourself, allowing the other person to say what is on his heart or mind.

2. **Spend three days in the tomb with Jesus.** When something really gets you upset and you

want to lash out in anger, remember that Jesus spent three days in the tomb. Wait three days before responding. During those three days, pray. Especially pray for the person you are angry with. You will be amazed to find that on the third day, you are not so upset with them anymore and can respond rationally, calmly, and lovingly.

3. **Spend time in silent prayer.** How often do we pray when we desperately need something from God? Prayers of petition are important. They acknowledge God's love and power. But they should not be our only form of prayer. To pray only when we need something is "vending machine" prayer. Let's try spending some time in quiet prayer when we are not asking or complaining about anything. Find a quiet spot or stop by the church for a visit. Pope Benedict XVI said that silence is "the sphere where God is born."[7]

CHAPTER 2

Listening to Others

It's very early morning, the sun just beginning to glint gold over the mountaintops, shadows of the night still covering the garden, lush with palms, cypress, and desert succulents. Mary Magdalene enters through the garden's low archway, her heart aching with desolation, eyes still red with weeping. To her astonishment, she finds the stone removed from the tomb, and she runs back to tell Simon Peter and John. "They have taken the Lord out of the tomb, and we do not know where they have laid him," she cries.

Upon returning to the tomb, they find it empty. And she remains there, weeping, while Peter and John go into the tomb to investigate. A man she at first takes to be the gardener asks her, "Woman, why are you weeping?"

"Sir, if you have carried him away, tell me where you have laid him, and I will take him away," she tells the man.

Jesus says to her, "Mary."

At this very moment, she recognizes him, calls him "Rabboni" (Teacher) and falls at his feet, grasping his clothing (John 20:2, 15,16).

Notice that she did not recognize him with her eyes, despite the fact that he bore the wounds of his crucifixion even in his glorified body. Rather, she recognized the *sound of his voice* as he spoke her name. "My sheep hear my voice, and I know them, and they follow me" (John 10:27).

Jesus speaks to each of us, calling our name.

He knows us more intimately than we know ourselves. When he calls our name, it resonates within the very depths of our soul. Indeed, this is because he is the God who formed us in the womb: "For you formed my inward parts; / you knitted me together in my mother's womb" (Psalm 139:13).

He calls our names, each one of us personally, to love and to share that love. Listen to Love. Listen, to love.

When we listen to others, we show that we love them. Listening puts the other person first. Listening allows the other to flower. Listening creates a space in which love can grow.

The Apostolate of the Ear

Pope Francis tells us that one of the main reasons he decided to proclaim a Holy Year of Mercy is that people today are in desperate need of mercy, and they are turning to many other — often ungodly — things in their search for it. He tells the interviewer, "Mostly, people are looking for someone to listen to them. Someone willing to grant them time, to listen to their dramas and difficulties. This is what I call the 'apostolate of the ear,' and it is important. Very important."[1]

Those who are in the front lines of evangelization will attest to the fact that so often, argumentation and reason — traditional apologetics — and even catechesis fail to bring their ex-Catholic or "none" family members and friends to the Faith. Sherry Weddell's influential book *Forming Intentional Disciples* addresses the fundamental reasons why our evangelization efforts are failing. A major problem is that we do not make the necessary personal connection at the outset. We can argue, quote Scripture, or cite dogma till we're blue in the face, and we will not win anyone over. She describes how, prior to any catechesis, there are thresholds of conversion that must occur within the future disciple of Jesus: trust, curiosity, openness, and seeking. The second threshold of conversion is "curiosity." "One of the best ways to rouse curiosity is to ask questions, not answer them."[2]

When we wish to draw our fallen-away sons and daughters or our spiritual-but-not-religious friends and relatives back to the Faith, it will not work to lecture, cajole, harass, or argue. Rather, it is when we truly listen to them, allow them to share the issues they are struggling with, that we become able to better answer their questions and hopefully meet their needs. "Often it is better simply to slow down," says Pope Francis, "to put aside our eagerness in order to see and listen to others, to stop rushing from one thing to another and to remain with someone who has faltered along the way."[3] We must practice the apostolate of the ear.

But not just with evangelization! It doesn't work to lecture, cajole, harass, or argue with our spouse and kids, either.

And listening becomes primary when we are trying to have better connections with our co-workers, neighbors, and estranged family members. Listening carefully to each other is the key to finding meaning, building solid friendships, and creating harmony in our close personal relationships. This is a true mercy.

Improving Our Relationships Through Listening

Austin* was a high-powered, successful lawyer who came to Art seeking counseling for his teenage son, whose mediocre grades and lack of interest in academics were becoming a source of daily conflict. The frustrated dad dragged the recalcitrant teen to the session. Dad was angry; son was sullen. Art listened while the dad vented. "I set everything up for James to succeed," he began. "All he has to do is his part. Show up. Pay attention in class, go to his tutoring session. He is never going to be successful in life with this attitude."

James was silent, withdrawn. Art requested separate sessions so that the son could feel free to speak his mind as well. It turned out that James had very different talents and aspirations — talents he felt his dad never acknowledged. He didn't want to be a lawyer like his dad. He was musically gifted, but

---

*All names, situations, and details in this book are fictitious composites of real situations that have been changed to protect the confidentiality of the individuals as well as to represent universal experiences.

his father had never heard him play. Instead, because Austin was so convinced that his son would follow in his footsteps, as he himself had done with his own father, he saw only his son's lack of motivation and success.

As long as Austin kept hammering away on the single theme of becoming a success (in the way he considered "success"), he would never discover where his son's passion and talents were. The more apathetic James got, the more his dad pressured him. Art's intervention was to reassure the father that the way to help his son begin to take charge of his life was not for the dad to do more, talk more, yell more, or pressure more but rather to take a step back, to give the son some space in which to share with his dad his own thoughts and feelings. Austin needed to give his son undivided attention and interest instead of constant commands for success. And then, he needed to listen. To listen empathically, which means that James was able to confirm that his dad had, indeed, understood what he was saying.

It may seem obvious to a third party, but we all do this from time to time. We are so focused on our own way of doing things or our own perspective on a situation that we actually miss what is really going on. In this case, the dad was so convinced that his son had to follow in his footsteps that he failed to perceive the reality his own son was facing. We may have the one child who, growing up, was always the class clown and the life of the party. We can't even imagine him growing serious and studying literature and philosophy. Yet, that is what happens when he goes away to college. Or we keep arguing with our spouse about finances, but he is feeling really pressured at work — and we aren't listening. We have to listen to understand who people are today and — most importantly — to love.

As Pope Francis wisely says,

> Instead of offering an opinion or advice, we need to be sure that we have heard everything the other person has to say. ... Often the other spouse does not need a solution to his or her problems, but simply to be heard, to feel that someone has acknowledged their pain, their disappointment, their fear, their anger, their hopes and their dreams.[4]

Preparing a Listening Heart

Before we give some practical suggestions about how to become a better listener, we want to talk about having a heart that is open to the other. Saint Teresa of Ávila used to say that before you pray, you have to remember to whom you are praying. This puts our heart in the right disposition. How many times have we rushed to Mass, speeding perhaps because we were running late, dashing in to find a seat, then quickly making the Sign of the Cross and automatically saying the prayers of the liturgy? And our minds were still whirling with all the things on our agenda that day or with that phone call we took as we were driving to church. Our hearts hadn't even begun to be in the proper place of reverence and openness to the Lord. When Moses caught sight of the burning bush, he turned to look. Once his attention was turned toward God, God called out to him from the bush; Moses took off his shoes, for it was holy ground.

When we engage in a conversation with someone, or prepare to really listen to a loved one, we ought, as Pope Francis says, to "remove our sandals before the sacred ground of the other (cf. Ex 3:5)."[5]

Listening is how we get to know another person. It's more than "straining to hear voices; it's about preparing the conditions of our hearts, cultivating an openness inside us. In this way, listening is a posture, one of availability and surrender."[6] Listening is more than a matter of technique. It is being open, interested, and radically available to the other. It is not a transaction, but an opportunity for transformation. So, first, let us open our hearts, clear our minds of presumptions, and turn toward the other with reverence.

The Fruit of Listening Is Joy

Henri Nouwen was a Dutch priest and author of more than forty books on the spiritual life, a beloved professor who taught at Notre Dame, Yale, and Harvard Divinity School. Yet, he never felt satisfied — in fact, he sometimes felt depressed — when working in the high-pressure, success-oriented environments of prestigious universities. He ultimately found himself at home at L'Arche, a community where able-bodied people live together with the disabled. Here he discovered profound lessons in the spiritual life. Instead of speaking all the time, instructing others, he grew by attending deeply to a severely disabled man named Adam. Every day he would bathe, dress, feed, and care for Adam for several hours. The time he spent with Adam became his most precious time of day. One day, a colleague of Nouwen's asked him: Is this what you got all that education for? And Nouwen realized that he experienced a greater joy in caring for Adam than he had ever experienced in his academic career.

Despite all his "upward mobility" — his speaking engagements, his teaching at prestigious universities, his successful career — he felt alone and depressed, anxious that someone might challenge his credentials. Then he realized that Christ's way is the way of "downward mobility" — the first shall be last; just as "the Son of Man came not to be served but to serve" (Matthew 20:28). Finally, at L'Arche, where he lived and served many with disabilities, he found joy and peace. "The joy that compassion brings is one of the best-kept secrets of humanity."[7]

This "secret" is what Father Nouwen discovered, and what many of us discover — whether through a gradual process of trial and error or through a trial by fire, in which we are thrown into a situation demanding much more compassionate self-giving than we had ever thought ourselves capable of. And we realize that what the world holds up as a successful and fulfilling life — power, money, prestige — paradoxically brings us less joy than the simple acts of humble self-giving. There is joy in listening.

Saint Paul, writing to the Galatians, compares the "works of the flesh" to the "fruit of the spirit." The latter are "love, joy, peace, patience, kindness, goodness, faithfulness, gentleness, self-control" (see Galatians 5:19–23).

Works of the flesh cause division, frustration, and lack of understanding. We participate in these works when we are competing with others to be first, wanting to have the last word or make the winning argument — and when we refuse to apologize or stubbornly insist on our own way of doing things. Or you may have erupted in anger when your spouse forgot to pick up that half-gallon of milk you requested. ("And now," you might have stormed, "there isn't any milk in the house!") Or maybe it was that time you had the brand-new daughter-in-law over for dinner and you couldn't resist arguing furiously with one of your adult children over whether psychological studies contain implicit biases and therefore cannot be trusted.

Listening, by contrast, brings joy.

Listening Is a Mercy

Kindness, patience, and listening lead to peace and joy, intimacy and love. You gain much more when you lose yourself. Lose yourself to silence, understanding, compassion. When the space between you and your loved ones is not filled with *you*, it can be filled with mercy and healing. Simply attending to the other, looking him or her in the eye, allows for this healing space.

This is love: Letting go of one's self in order to allow the other to bloom, to reveal himself or herself. As Pope Francis says in *Amoris Laeticia*: "Those who love not only refrain from speaking too much about themselves, but are focused on others; they do not need to be the center of attention."[8] Love is self-gift and also self-surrender. We willingly abandon ourselves to the other, to be gift as Jesus gave himself in abandonment to the Father.

— **PRACTICAL APPLICATION** —

We are going to build on our practical application from the last chapter. In that exercise, our task was to remain silent in a situation in which we really *wanted* to respond: instead of jumping in with a comment, correction, or solution, we paused in silence. We compared this time of silence to the three days that Christ spent in the tomb.

In this exercise, we are going to practice empathy.

Can empathy be taught?

You may think that empathy is something you have or you don't, like a natural talent. Some people seem to be naturally empathic. But recent studies have shown that empathy can be taught. Researchers asked whether teaching empathy could help decrease school bullying, improve medical professionals' bedside manner, or help engineering students relate to others. In one study at the University of Georgia,[9] students who came from upper-middle-class families role-played living in an impoverished family — having to find shelter, provide food and clothing, and take care of their children while dealing with constraints such as language barriers and lack of transportation. At the end of the study, it was found that the students did show an increase in empathy. So, in this exercise, we are going to improve our empathy!

Before the exercise, let's look at an example. In the following, which response is empathic to this statement?

"I am sick and tired of everyone at work complaining all the time!"

    a. "Me, too! I'm surrounded by cranky kids all day!"

    b. "You're probably responsible for the attitude at work."

    c. "Why don't you try having a team-building activity offsite?"

    d. "You must be so frustrated!" (Response "d" is empathic, but the best response will be not only empathic but also encouraging further discussion.)

    e. "You must be so frustrated! *Why do you think that is?*"

We are so often tempted to provide a solution, responding with our own similar struggles or stories. This is well intentioned, an attempt to find common ground and to be empathic. However, it only shifts the attention to ourselves and can result in the other person feeling discounted.

Another common error is to think that what is needed is an immediate solution to the problem. Men are often accused of being advice-givers; it is possibly related to their wanting to protect and defend, and not really knowing how to respond other than suggesting a solution. But often this only serves to stifle the conversation. The other person may not want advice or a solution; she may need to "vent." She doesn't feel understood. And, even if she *does* want advice, she *first* wants to feel understood.

Finally, some responses are blaming; perhaps by temperament we are the sort of people who like to solve our own problems, thinking that complaining is "whining." So we project that onto the ones we are listening to, blaming them for their own problems. This is the least empathic response.

Empathy does not require agreement or feeling the same way as the other person. It does entail *understanding* how the other feels and conveying that understanding. And it makes it more likely that the other person will respond empathically as well.

Exercise

Choose a partner and have this person pick an *imaginary problem or issue* that he will want you to express empathy about.

It is important that this be an *imaginary* topic, to reduce any potential defensiveness. Your partner will complain, and you will express empathy. You will convince your partner that you have understood. Use the principles explained and illustrated above, and use the following conversations as models.

> **Partner:** "I was really upset the way you dressed up like a clown and jumped out of the bushes to frighten me yesterday!"
>
> **You:** "You were really frightened?"
>
> **Partner:** "Yes, and I am angry about it too."
>
> **You:** "I'm sorry that I frightened and angered you. You must have really been upset with me."
>
> **Partner:** "Yes! I was scared and also angry at you for doing that to me."
>
> **You:** "I understand now that you were scared and angry. Is there anything else I am missing?"
>
> **Partner:** "I don't want you ever to do that again."
>
> **You:** "You were scared and angry, and you want me to promise that I will never do that again."

This simple example has the key elements of empathy:

- Listening for the emotion expressed and the point of view.

- Demonstrating to the partner that you really heard him and really understood what the partner said and is feeling.
- Checking out that he feels empathically understood ("Yes! I was scared....")

Once you get this down, then try a real-life example. The challenge with a real-life example is that the temptation to be defensive, argumentative, or to "straighten out his misconceptions" will be very strong. Pray for self-control. You want to understand; not to be understood. You want to understand the other, not win an argument or make a point. You want to express empathy to the other's satisfaction. That's the loving, listening task at hand.

You: "I want to practice empathy on a real topic that I know has bothered you. Is now a good time?"

Partner: "Yes, it is."

You: "Thanks. I know you have been upset about how often I come home from work and arrive late for dinner. Can you tell me how you feel about that, and let's see if I can really understand to your satisfaction?"

Partner: "Sure. Are you ready?"

You: "Yes. Fire away." (And tell yourself: I will not get defensive. I will not get defensive....)

Partner: "Even though we have agreed to have dinner together, you still put your work first, and you often come home late. It makes me wonder how much we really matter to you."

You: (fighting the urge to be defensive or unfairly judged) "Okay. You are not just bothered but get very angry with me when I come home in the middle of dinner. And more than that, it makes you wonder if I am really committed to being with you, because you fear that I think more highly of work than of our relationship. Did I get that right?" (Stay calm. Focus on seeing if you really understood.)

Partner: "That's very close. This has bothered me for a long time."

You: "I understand that this has been painful for you for quite a while and it is very disturbing to you. You are probably pretty angry with me."

Partner: "Yes. I am."

You: "Earlier you said that I am close to understanding. Is there something I am missing?"

Partner: "Just that I was afraid that you were not as committed to me as I was to you. That also made me very upset and even afraid for our relationship."

You: "So the fear was that I wasn't really committed to the relationship, and that was evidenced by my often being late for dinner because of work duties."

Partner: "Yes. That's the fear."

You can see how hard it is not to be defensive. Maybe it's traffic, maybe a difficult boss, maybe the workload is unbearable, and so on. Those things can, if necessary, come out later when, ideally, your partner listens to you with empathy. But for now, this empathy has allowed a deep hurt to be disclosed. It's more than just a cold dinner; it's a relationship that is in trouble. Empathy can disclose that and start the healing. Once empathy has been reached, then you can start discussing problem-solving:

- I'll try to get home on time and deal with work issues from my computer at home after dinner.
- I'll have a talk with my boss to let him know that at least three days a week I must leave at 4:30 but will take calls on the way home.
- I'll come to work early the next day to address issues when my family is asleep and it doesn't cause domestic stress, etc.

After empathy, solutions can be found.

CHAPTER 3

Listening to Your Heart

Several years ago, Laraine got a frantic call from her mom. "I need you to come home right now, because I think your dad is dying." Now, Laraine and her mother lived on opposite ends of the country, her parents in Nevada and we in Virginia. They spoke weekly on the phone, and she had just recently returned from a visit.

Thinking her mom might simply be overreacting, Laraine asked for more details. "Are you sure? He seemed okay when I was there two weeks ago!" Laraine put in a call to her dad's doctor. "How is he, really? Do I need to fly out now?"

The doctor replied, "No, he is doing well. He's home, recovering from pneumonia, and he is on oxygen — but he is not in danger of dying!" Despite these reassurances, Laraine's mom insisted that she "just knew." So Laraine flew out to Nevada and visited with her dad. It wasn't more than a week later that he did, in fact, have a sudden relapse, was rushed to the hospital in an ambulance, and after a few days, passed away. If Laraine's mom had not listened to her heart, and if Laraine had not listened to *her* heart, she would have missed visiting with him one last time.

What is the heart? The *Catechism of the Catholic Church* tells us that God *touches our hearts* through the illumination of the Holy Spirit (CCC 1993). Further,

> The heart is our hidden center, beyond the grasp of our reason and of others; only the Spirit of God can fathom the human heart and know it fully. The heart is the place of decision, deeper than our psychic drives. It is the place of truth, where we choose life or death. It is the place of encounter, because as image of God we live in relation: it is the place of covenant. (CCC 2563)

The place of truth, the place of encounter, the place of covenant. This is pretty mystical-sounding! Yet, we instinctively know that the heart is our "hidden center" — it is the heart that loves, that desires, that is compassionate, that mourns. We even say that the heart "knows," though we mean a more intuitive sort of knowing. Our deepest emotions come from our heart: we experience heartfelt sorrow upon a loved one's passing, our heart aches when we are estranged from a loved one. Someone who is cruel or mistreats people is "heartless." It is our heart that feels the loss or gain of relationships. And it is from the heart that good or evil comes (Matthew 15:10–20; Mark 7:14–23).

When the Pharisees object that Jesus' disciples have not washed their hands, Christ explains that it is not what goes into a man that defiles him but what *comes from his heart*. "For out of the heart come evil thoughts, murder, adultery, fornication, theft, false witness, slander. These are what defile a man" (Matthew 15:19–20). Our deepest passions — love, hatred, desire — arise from our heart. In a certain sense, the heart is the true core of the person, with mysterious depths even we sometimes fail to fathom. This is why we plead along with the psalmist, "Create in me a clean heart, O God" (Psalm 51:10), and why Christ wanted to manifest his love for us through the image of the Sacred Heart. God knows how easily our hearts can wander, and he wants to give us his own heart to infuse and inflame ours with his love: "A new heart I will give you, and a new spirit I will put within you; and I will take out of your flesh the heart of stone ..." (Ezekiel 36:26).

Pharaoh's Hard Heart

A number of years ago, one of our daughter's best friends ("Ari") began attending a local Catholic high school because it had a strong academic reputation. Ari was of Indian descent, and her grandparents were Sikhs, though her parents were not practicing. The high school required a class on the Old Testament, and father was reading the assignments alongside his daughter. One day, when we were visiting, Ari's father asked: "I don't understand this part. It says, 'The LORD hardened Pharaoh's heart' [Exodus 9:12 and see Exodus 9:30] so that he wouldn't let the people go; yet it was the Lord who wanted Moses to ask Pharaoh to let the people go. How can God, who is all-good, cause someone else to sin?"

Laraine was stumped. She went back to the text, and noticed that before God hardened Pharaoh's heart, Pharaoh himself hardened his heart (Exodus 7:13, 7:22, 8:15). After every plague that was sent, Pharaoh either became obstinate or hardened his own heart. Therefore, God is not directly willing evil nor is he directly forcing someone to sin. He is permitting Pharaoh's own will.

Saint Paul, in Romans 9, tackles this very difficult question:

> What then are we to say? Is there injustice upon the part of God? Of course not! For he says to Moses:
>
> > "I will show mercy to whom I will,
> > I will take pity on whom I will."
>
> So it depends not upon a person's will or exertion, but upon God, who shows mercy. For the scripture says to Pharaoh, "This is why I have raised you up, to show my power through you that my name may be proclaimed throughout the earth." Consequently, he has mercy upon whom he wills, and he hardens whom he wills. (Romans 9:14–18, NABRE)

Though this may sound capricious on God's part, it points to the fundamental tension between God's plan for salvation and the invitation to love him in freedom: "Behold, I stand at the door and knock" (Revelation 3:20) — he does not force himself upon us but draws us with bands of love to the heavenly banquet. "He set me free in the open; / he rescued me because he loves me" (Psalm 18:20, NABRE).

Pharaoh had numerous opportunities to repent and to allow the Israelites to leave. In a sense, Pharaoh's story is not unlike each of our own paths through life. How many times does God allow us to repent of our sins and turn toward him once again? How many times do we harden our own hearts against his will? Yet each time, he allows us to return again to him. This story will be repeated until we come to the end of our lives; at some point, there will be no further opportunities for conversion of our hearts. Perhaps this is what the final "hardening of Pharaoh's heart" represents: our final opportunity before we walk through the door to eternity. Thus, Pharaoh's hard heart is a cautionary tale for each one of us.

A hardened heart will not be able to listen well, neither to God nor to others. "Oh, that today you would hear his voice, / Harden not your hearts" (Hebrews 3:8, NABRE).

It is vital for our relationships with God and others to strive to know our hearts, to turn our hearts toward God, to purify our hearts: "Blessed are the pure in heart, for they shall see God" (Matthew 5:8). For our own peace of mind and strength of soul, we need to ponder the teaching of our faith that our heart is the place "to which I withdraw" (CCC 2563).

The Withdrawing Room

Have you ever had one of those days when you felt pulled in a hundred different directions — emotionally, spiritually, maybe even physically — and you felt completely unmoored, with no sense of where *you* really are? All are demanding something of you or complaining that you aren't answering their needs ... and you are feeling stretched beyond your limits. To top it off, you are lost in the middle of it all.

At times like these, we believe there is nothing better than to "withdraw to your inner room" and turn to Jesus in prayer. We find it especially consoling and centering to spend quiet time in the chapel in front of the Blessed Sacrament. There, enveloped by stillness and peace, the confusion and demands of the world slowly drop away as we enter into the presence of the Lord.

Even if we can't physically get to church or to make a visit to a Blessed Sacrament chapel, we can withdraw to our inner room. Our lives are so hectic, so filled with noise, with multiple demands on our attention and time, that we desperately need silence in order to collect ourselves. We need to spend time in silence. Without this time, we are likely to become more and more brittle and fragile, resentful of all the demands on our time and energy, lacking the interior strength that comes from prayer.

Saint Teresa of Ávila, mystic and doctor of the Church, compares the soul to a beautiful diamond castle with many rooms. So many people never enter their interior castle. Instead, they roam around outside the castle in the darkness, where the reptiles and poisonous vermin lurk. The door to the interior castle, where God dwells within, is prayer.

This is not to say that you will receive immediate answers every time you pray — especially if your mind and emotions are in serious turmoil — but you will begin to experience that peace that only Christ can give. "Peace I leave with you; my peace I give to you; not as the world gives do I give to you. Let not your hearts be troubled, neither let them be afraid" (John 14:27).

Sometimes, the peace we think we need is "peace and quiet" or the peace of an immediate answer. Yet the peace of Christ does not depend on the absence of conflict. Our Lord brings peace to our souls in spite of the strife and turmoil of our world. Sometimes we are looking for a solution to a particular conundrum of our lives — perhaps we are trying to fix a broken relationship or we can't figure out the next step for our career. We may be feeling swamped by bills or dealing with an aging parent who needs caregiving. In all these situations, God speaks to our hearts in silence.

The psalmist writes, "I bless the LORD who gives me counsel; / in the night also my heart instructs me" (Psalm 16:7). The Divine Physician can console and direct our heart, healing all its hidden wounds.

Wounds of the Heart

Sister Elizabeth Wagner is an award-winning writer, spiritual director, and hermit. She tells of a pilgrimage she made to the shrine of Saint Anne de Beaupré in Quebec. She paused to pray, alone, at the altar of Saint Anne. Suddenly, she found herself overcome by a deep sadness, and she began sobbing uncontrollably; "I never had a grandmother!" she realized. She had never thought of this before, yet in front of the statue of Saint Anne she became aware of a big hole in her heart. "Suddenly, unexpectedly, my heart had opened, and I was standing within," she writes.[1]

What a wonderful, yet unusual experience: to discover her deepest self, even though at first she found it a place of grief and misery. She pondered the mysterious discovery of grief and loss that she hadn't even known she was carrying in her heart. She writes:

What happened at St. Anne's? What brought up this knowledge of my heart? No doubt it was the blessed stillness and spaciousness, which allowed my heart to surrender its wound. What enabled me to perceive and understand? It was all the years of working to find and live from my heart.[2]

We don't find it unusual that a contemplative nun (and hermit!) would spend years searching within, developing a deep interior life, growing in quiet self-knowledge, seeking out times and seasons in which she can grow inward in silence and understanding.

But we are too busy, right?

Wrong. We, too, need to develop the interior life, grow in self-knowledge and understanding — to "find and live from" our heart. Our Faith is an inside-out faith. Not only must we love God with all our heart, soul, and mind *before* we love ourselves, but also we must go into our inner room and pray to God in secret so that our Father who sees in secret will repay us (Matthew 6:4). If we do not develop our interior life, not only will our souls resemble parched earth in which no seeds could take root, we may also make some serious mistakes in our daily lives.

Attending to the Heart

"Andrea" was a twentysomething who was just beginning her professional career, graduating with a Bachelor of Science in nursing. Her family was thrilled, especially her mom, when she began dating a young Catholic man. Andrea had been a serious student throughout college and had not yet had a serious relationship. Her mom had been exerting pressure on Andrea to "find a nice young Catholic man" and to marry young. Andrea met "Derek" at a church event, and he seemed to have all the "credentials" — he was good-looking, agreed with her on important issues, was intelligent, and had a professional career.

Things were moving very quickly — perhaps too quickly for Andrea — but not quickly enough for her mom. Her mom had already started scouting reception venues and was suggesting bridal gowns and bakers. Derek was invited to many family functions and seemed to fit in perfectly. He dramatically proposed on the beach at sunset while a hidden photographer waited to snap the perfect engagement photos. Andrea was swept up by the contagious enthusiasm of her family and friends. Six months later, they were married, despite the fact that Andrea had spent the evening before the wedding battling an anxiety attack that threatened to ruin the rehearsal dinner. Her mom reassured her, "These are typical wedding nerves! We all go through this!"

It was only after the wedding that everything fell apart. Aspects of Derek's personality that he had managed to hide during their engagement were revealed. And the nagging suspicion that something wasn't right — which Andrea had squelched throughout their whirlwind engagement — became a full-blown nightmare. He was addicted to pornography, verbally abusive, and violently angry at times.

Andrea knew she should have taken time to listen to her heart instead of listening to the world.

The Answer Comes from Within

Sometimes, when we are trying very hard to please someone or live up to a particular image we have of ourselves, we may jump through hoops and even appear quite successful — yet all the while, internally, we are battling serious doubts.

Dolores Hart was a young, rising Hollywood star, having made her film debut with Elvis Presley in the movie *Loving You*. She had always wanted to be an actress and to marry and have a family. Yet she stunned Hollywood when she left at the peak of her career to answer the call she heard with "the ear of the heart":

> I want so desperately to run away from this place — but to where? Back to the wasting of moment to moment, awaiting the temporal alleviation of boredom by trivial excitement? No, I must stay here and wait for another signpost. Listen, you fool. But to what am I listening?
>
> I pondered the strange new awakening in my heart that cried for explanation.[3]

This was an entry in Dolores' diary on one of her visits to the Regina Laudis monastery in Connecticut. She was confused by her lack of fulfillment in her beloved career, acting — she had always wanted to be an actress, and she was much lauded and at the height of her career. Even Peter Sellers threw himself at her in a blatant attempt to seduce her.

She was dating a man she felt very comfortable with, someone she admired and respected. They had taken a break in their relationship while she was filming a movie, because she had been reluctant to move forward. When she returned, she wrote a letter to the Mother Superior at Regina Laudis, say-

ing that she wanted to discuss the possibility of a vocation. Just
as she was going to mail the letter, she ran into her boyfriend,
who invited her out to dinner. She was thrilled to see him
again, so she stuffed the letter into her purse. That evening,
Don asked her to marry him and she agreed, if they could
be secretly engaged for six months. The newspapers somehow
found out, and they were forced to set a date publicly.

As the wedding date drew near, Dolores felt more and
more conflicted. One night her fiancé asked her whether she
was still thinking about the monastery and urged her to resolve the question once and for all. Dolores couldn't understand how she could be struggling over a potential vocation
when the wedding invitations had been printed, she was under contract for a new film, and acting was the career she had
always dreamed of!

Dolores had spent months resisting the call from God, because it didn't fit what she thought she wanted in her life. Yet
she felt frustrated and unfulfilled when she was away from the
monastery, pursuing her career. She wanted Mother Benedict
to tell her what to do, but the nun continued to insist that
Dolores must find the answer within her own heart: "You will
find the will of God when you find what it is in your own
heart that you know you must do. ... Don't look for God
in some abstraction. The answer comes from within yourself,
Dolores. What is it that you want?"[4]

Dolores Hart decided to break off her engagement and
ask permission to enter the monastery. She became a contemplative Benedictine nun, and for more than fifty years the
Abbey of Regina Laudis has been her home.

Discovering the Depths of the Heart

Certain experiences — a deep and ardent love, sublime joy upon entering a majestic cathedral or listening to a beautiful symphony or viewing a breathtaking snowy mountain range against crystal blue sky — come to us as pure gift. We cannot create these experiences for ourselves (in fact, sometimes we misuse created things like alcohol or sex or drugs or money to try to create the experience of transcendent happiness we desire). Dietrich Von Hildebrand tells us that these affective responses come from a mysterious place, the very depths of our soul, the most intimate part of ourselves — the heart. Such happiness is pure gift, "dropping like dew upon our heart, shining gratuitously like a sunray into our soul."[5]

All men seek happiness, in ways that are often misguided. But true happiness (as opposed to passing sensory pleasure) is a gift. It is not something we can achieve by our own power. It is a gift.

What makes you truly happy? Not just the short-lived, pleasure-type happiness of having a delicious ice cream sundae or the tantalizing happiness that comes from being powerful or lauded, but the deep-down, pure-bliss happiness, like the day you held your firstborn child or when you stood at the top of a mountain as the sun glinted off snow-topped peaks and absorbed the stunning beauty of God's creation.

As we withdraw to our true dwelling place, our innermost room, the interior castle, we seek to plumb the depths of our own hearts, yet we may find that it takes years to discover all the mysteries therein. It is a lifelong project, and as Saint Teresa of Ávila said, even if she were drawn to the highest heavens, she would not want to cease her quest for self-knowledge.[6]

— PRACTICAL APPLICATION —

John Gottman, Ph.D., and his wife, Julie Schwartz Gottman, Ph.D., have been researching what makes marriages work for decades. They have watched happy couples and unhappy couples talk to each other, discuss problems, and even fight. They have followed the couples to see which ones divorced and which stayed happily married. They have counted the number of times spouses rolled their eyeballs or leaned toward the other to touch their shoulder. With decades of thorough research under their belts, the Gottmans are in a position to be able to identify what types of communication keep relationships strong. One of these principles was to discover the dreams within the conflict. This requires listening to your heart and listening to your loved one's heartfelt dreams.

"Until dreams and feelings are recognized and honored, the conflict is going to keep resurfacing in ways that are often frustrating and sometimes painful."[7] The Gottmans suggest going deeper to uncover the issues our loved one may be dealing with and to acknowledge each other's dreams. You can ask questions such as: "Why is this important to you?"; "Is there some story behind this that I should understand?"; "Can you tell me all your feelings about this?"; or "Is there a deeper purpose or goal in this for you?"

A number of years ago, out of the blue, Art announced that he wanted to go backpacking in the wilderness. The kind where you are dropped by a helicopter into the middle of nowhere on a mountaintop and you have to find your way out, guided only by the stars. Laraine immediately snorted, "That's insane!"

And, if you know Art, you know that this is true. The last time we went camping we couldn't get the coffee to percolate on the Coleman stove, so we left the kids in their tents and drove off to the nearest Starbucks. Yet the first thing out of Laraine's mouth should not have been scornful. This effectively shut down all conversation on the topic. What she should have said was, "Tell me why this is important to you?"

That simple question would have furthered conversation and deepened her understanding of Art's hopes and dreams. It would have drawn her closer to his heart.

Exercise

Take turns being the listener and the speaker. Speakers tell the listeners about their dreams or goals or frustrations. And the listeners draw information out of the other by asking questions such as: *What is important to you about this dream? What is the most important part? Why is this part important? Is there a story behind this for you? Tell me that story. Tell me all the feelings you have about this dream. Are there any feelings you left out? How do you imagine things would be if you got what you wanted? Do you have any fears about not having this dream honored?*[8]

CHAPTER 4

Listening to Criticism

The First Horseman of the Apocalypse

Listening to criticism is one of the most difficult things for us social animals. According to Dr. John Gottman, criticism is one of the harbingers of marriage failure — the first of the "four horsemen of the apocalypse." It is marriage poison. So let's begin our reflection on listening to criticism with handling complaints in marriage as a case study.

Now we all criticize on occasion. Everyone — even the most loving couples — must express a complaint here and there. Of course, every marriage has disagreements! Marriage partners need to be able to express their concerns, their *legitimate* complaints. A healthy marriage involves respectfully discussing problems.

Avoiding problems and concerns leads to stockpiling grievances, keeping track of every offense, and either suddenly exploding like a dirty bomb or else experiencing "negative sentiment override." That occurs when bad feelings overwhelm good ones. Everything looks and feels bad.[1]

But a steady diet of criticism leads to defensiveness in our partner and eventually brings on the remaining three horsemen — and ultimately marital distress. In their research, the Gottmans found that criticism caused a spike in heart rate, blood pressure, and other stress-related symptoms. These result in a "fight or flight" scenario — usually on the part of the male. In the unhappy relationships, there was a vicious cycle of nagging, criticism, and complaints by the wife, followed by withdrawal and stonewalling by the husband.

There are good ways and bad ways to express our complaints. We can state our complaints in a reasonable, loving fashion. Thus, the Gottmans distinguish the legitimate expression of problems or complaints from *unconstructive* criticism.

By "criticism," the Gottmans mean statements like the following: "You never come home on time!" or "You are dragging us down with your spending!" Criticism is attacking the other *person* rather than attacking the *problem*. When we blame or yell something like "You're such a workaholic! You never come home for dinner on time!" or "You're just like your father!" we are generalizing about the other person's *character*, rather than focusing on a single issue. And the other person is not likely to take kindly to what we are saying. He will likely become defensive and argue back, "Well if you cooked a decent dinner once in a while, maybe I would!" or "That's not true that I NEVER come home for dinner! I did just last week!" In any case, a divisive situation has been created, a conflict in which both spouses are angry, hurt, and defensive, attacking *each other* rather than the problem at hand.

There are ways of bringing up problems that lead to further discussion and, ultimately, resolution. In our book *The Temperament God Gave Your Spouse*, we discuss constructive ways to address problems without blaming or causing defensiveness. We have many communication tips that help couples discuss problems in responsible, loving ways, such as the "softened start-up," expressing the underlying positive and the principle of five-to-one.

But in this chapter, we are focusing on *listening* to criticism:

At the end of your life you will groan,
    when your flesh and body are spent.
You will say, "How I hated discipline!
    How my heart spurned correction!
I would not obey my teachers
    or turn my ear to my instructors.
And I was soon in serious trouble
    in the assembly of God's people."
(Proverbs 5:11-14, NIV)

Yet …

[C]orrection and instruction
    are the way to life.
(Proverbs 6:23)

We can all relate to the words from Scripture, "How I hated discipline! How my heart spurned correction!" Why is criticism so hard to hear?

Listening to criticism is tremendously difficult. We all have wounds that can become inflamed by criticism. It is especially difficult for those who are sensitive by nature. Depending on temperament,[2] some people tend to react angrily when criticized, and respond by attacking the critic. For example, if your spouse says, "I can tell from our checkbook that you've been spending more than we budgeted for groceries this month," your response might be: "Well, you shouldn't talk! You're always going out for expensive lunches!" Others do not respond outwardly but feel deeply wounded and the criticism festers over time, resulting in deep resentment. For still others, the criticism may wash off their back like water off a duck.

Knowing Our Temperament

How do we tend to respond? As a choleric, Laraine's preferred temperamental response is to become argumentative, angry, and go on the offensive. "Oh, yeah? Well who are you to criticize me?" Art, as an introverted phlegmatic, is more likely to soak in the criticism and brood about it for days, alternating between resentment and self-chastisement.

Knowing our temperament is an important step in being prepared to listen. Temperament is how we tend, instinctively, to react. If we know how we *tend* to react, we can mentally prepare ourselves in situations where we know we are likely to face criticism — for example, at work or with our spouse.

One of the greatest treatises ever written on the spiritual life — *The Spiritual Life*, by Father Adolphe Tanquerey, written in 1930 — sums up the necessity of self-knowledge (and in particular knowing one's temperament): "If we lack self-knowledge, it is morally impossible to perfect ourselves." And this, because we tend to harbor illusions about ourselves. Depending on temperament, these fall into one of two categories: "We fall either into a *presumptuous optimism* that makes us believe we are already perfect, or into *discouragement* that causes us to exaggerate our faults."[3]

The extraverted temperaments (choleric, sanguine) tend to presumptuous optimism while the introverted temperaments (melancholic, phlegmatic) tend to discouragement. These will be particularly noticeable when responding to criticism. In either case, we must challenge ourselves to listen to the criticism and to remain as receptive as possible, falling neither into presumption nor into discouragement.

The extraverted choleric is quick to react, tends to assume he is always right, and responds to criticism aggressively and even angrily by immediately going on the offensive. Think sportscaster Colin Cowherd.

The introverted melancholic is slow to respond, but when she does, her reaction is intense and internal. She will brood about it for days, chastising or berating herself, wondering how she could have done better, wishing she would have responded better to the criticism, becoming more and more resentful of the one who criticized her. The criticism becomes overblown in her mind and a festering wound to the soul.

As an introvert, the phlegmatic doesn't respond immediately either but is much more able to hear the criticism. The impression doesn't go as deep as the melancholic but is nonetheless taken to heart and can lead to self-criticism and loss of confidence.

The extraverted sanguine tends to respond immediately, perhaps emotionally. She may cry or react with nervous laughter, or try to turn the whole thing into a joke. She wants to be liked and admired, and criticism embarrasses her, but she will try to win you over with her eagerness to please. She will not brood over the criticism but will quickly forgive and forget.

Knowing our temperament helps us prepare to listen and to understand. As a choleric-sanguine, Laraine would have to remind herself that she needs to tone down the reaction, to hear the other person out, and to keep strong judgments at bay. Art, as a phlegmatic-melancholic, needs to remind himself that one critical comment doesn't mean his entire life is a disaster; he has to keep the criticism he is hearing within the scope of the situation and not generalize it or blow it out of proportion.

Men and Women Respond Differently

The Gottmans measured heart rates and observed signs of distress during the middle of an argument or sensitive discussion.

Men would quickly reach a high threshold and go into "flight or fight" mode — they simply couldn't handle the stress. Feeling overwhelmed by the onslaught of negativity causes what the Gottmans dubbed "flooding." Men are particularly prone to flooding, which is why you often find men withdrawing into stony silences or avoiding discussing anything that might remotely result in potential criticism. They might even spend hours of free time golfing or watching sports or otherwise distancing themselves to avoid any negative feelings. If flooding becomes a chronic state, it is likely to result in serious marital distress.[4]

"Why Don't You Love Me?"

Whatever our instinctive reaction, most of us feel hurt by criticism. This makes us feel defensive and abandon listening.

It is likely that criticism strikes at our fundamental desire to be loved. We all want to be loved, respected, and appreciated, and criticism seems in the moment to be the opposite. Of course, a parent will say that he must criticize the child because he loves him. "Correction and instruction are the way to life" (Proverbs 6:23, NIV) and "the Lord disciplines him whom he loves" (Hebrews 12:6).

Yet we don't feel that way in the midst of being criticized. There are many reasons we feel especially hurt or angry when hearing criticism. One factor is the *way* the criticism is given — especially if the other person is directly attacking our character or is particularly clumsy in the way he or she presents the critical point. (Again, there are many ways to bring up problems that will diminish the feeling of being attacked, that will make it clear that we are loved.)

Another factor is our own emotional state. We may be feeling particularly hormonal, or sad, or under stress. Sometimes, the person criticizing us is someone we have recently been trying desperately to please. Sometimes, the criticism pokes an old wound.

Let's look at an example.

Sandra and Marcia worked together in a small office. Usually they worked on their own projects, but whenever a new direct-mail brochure needed to be created, they collaborated. By temperament, Marcia was sales-oriented, enthusiastic, and energetic, coming up with clever captions and slogans. Sandra was serious, methodical, and attentive to detail. With their opposite strengths to balance each other out, they made the perfect team.

Except when they didn't.

Their opposite temperaments sometimes got in the way of smooth communication. Marcia would complain that Sandra was altogether too nitpicky. Sandra would point out that if she hadn't been so "picky," they would have lost the account.

During one particularly testy interchange, Sandra had a near meltdown over what Marcia considered a minor grammar disagreement over a comma. And Marcia had a sudden realization that there was something underneath all the angst and the emotionality — something deeper than a mere temperament conflict. She suspected that in Sandra's past, there had been bullying or disrespect, such that her own lighthearted and somewhat impulsive personality was causing painful memories to arise. Marcia resolved to listen more carefully when Sandra made a comment and not to disagree instantly when Sandra had a correction to make.

In this example, conflict and constructive criticism paved the way for a deeper understanding. Marcia first needed to be open to listening to criticism — and even hearing something that was hidden within.

Though criticism brings out very natural feelings of anger, resentment, or embarrassment (and feelings are never wrong in themselves; it is how we act on them that may be sinful), we have one of two ways we can go: we can act on those feelings or we can let them go and try to "rise above" them, as they say. This is very liberating.

Another excellent reason to become more adept at taking criticism is that it helps us grow in holiness. Our response to criticism often reveals our humility — or lack thereof! Yet criticism is an opportunity to grow in this important virtue.

The Foundation of All Virtues

Humility is the virtue without which no other virtue can be acquired. It is foundational, the ground, and the word comes from the Latin *humus* — of the earth. It is not denigrating ourselves, being a doormat. It is not thinking that *we* are dirt. It is not thinking less of ourselves. Rather, it is thinking of ourselves less. It is having a more accurate assessment of ourselves, an appreciation for where we stand in relation to God, who is Truth. Saint Augustine says, "Humility is the foundation of all the other virtues; hence, in the soul in which this virtue does not exist, there cannot be any other virtue except in mere appearance."

During Lent in 2017, both of us went on pilgrimage to the Holy Land. When we visited Bethlehem and the Church of the Nativity, we had to enter through a door that was four feet high and about two feet wide. It is called the Door of Humility. It reminds pilgrims that Jesus Christ entered the world as a helpless baby. God lowered himself to be born as a man, to suffer and die.

John Climacus lived in the seventh century as a monk at the foot of Mount Sinai, where Moses received the Ten Commandments from God himself. He was known as John of the Ladder, after his famous book *The Ladder of Divine Ascent*. He was so respected as a spiritual guide that he received many visits from fellow monks seeking his counsel. Some monks who were envious of his popularity accused him of being a chatterbox and a gossip. At this, Saint John kept total silence for an entire year, until his very critics begged him to speak once again. In this particular case, the future saint was being unjustly criticized; yet he took it as an opportunity to grow in heroic virtue.

There are many examples of saints accepting unfounded criticism. Saint Teresa of Ávila was notably *mis*instructed by spiritual directors who were far less qualified than she, yet she was obedient to them. She was even investigated by the Church. We do not have to respond this way to unfounded or unjust criticism; yet, practicing restraint will afford us growth in virtue.

Being Open to the Truth

Laraine once had a work situation in which there was a rather overbearing, supercilious manager who seemed obsessed with small issues. If someone left something on the copier, entered his office without knocking, or failed to triple-check a purchase order, this petty dictator would scold and make note of the transgressions for your performance evaluation.

At first, Laraine's approach was rather combative. She figured that this person needed standing up to; he was an office bully, and Laraine's self-appointed job was protector of the staff, especially those who were more timid.

But one day, Laraine had an interesting experience. One of her rather soft-spoken co-workers gently admonished her after a rather rousing debate had occurred between Laraine and the overbearing boss. In Laraine's mind she had been calmly, dispassionately standing up to tyrannical nonsense. Her quiet office mate said, "You know, Laraine, you might consider not escalating." Laraine was stunned. Was that what she had been doing? She thought she was Defending the Innocent and Protecting the Weak. Her self-image did not match someone who escalates hostilities. This gave her pause and was an opportunity to reflect.

We sometimes have a self-image that is not aligned with reality. When we are criticized, our self-image (or the image we wish to project) is threatened. This may bring up past wounds or may simply make us feel embarrassed. The more the defenses we have built up, the more difficult it will be to accept the criticism. And the thickest fortress is necessary for those areas that bring up painful wounds or shameful feelings.

It makes us stop and wonder: Why are we not completely transparent — to ourselves and to others? Why are there hidden parts, parts we are ashamed of, lies we tell ourselves, fantasies we dream about, games we play? It is very difficult to listen to constructive criticism, but it is often necessary.

The Hidden Corners

A spiritual master, Father Frederick William Faber, who wrote "Faith of Our Fathers" and many other beautiful hymns, spent much time in his book *Spiritual Conferences* discussing self-deceit. He said that self-deceit "is perhaps the most uncomfortable and disquieting subject in the whole of spiritual theology. ... It is not easy to know ourselves. On the contrary, it is the hardest thing in the world." He added, "There is hardly a man or woman in the world who has not got some corner of self into which he or she fears to venture with a light."

It's an instinct, perhaps a vestige of that original sin (when Adam said, "She made me do it!" and Eve blamed the serpent, with neither of them taking responsibility for their own actions). We keep this corner of our self locked up, like a hidden closet where dirt and disorder are piling up. Or, as one priest once described in a hilariously vivid image: We are sitting contentedly on the front porch of our mountain cabin, drinking tea and watching the sunset; meanwhile, a bear comes rampaging in through the back door, wreaking havoc and carrying off all our food. Whether through laziness or pride, we are ignorant of what is going on inside our own house.

We offer excuses for our own behavior; we think that, in our case, we have extenuating circumstances that make something less wrong for us than for others — whether it is temperament ("I can't help it if I'm high strung!") or health ("My hormones are raging right now!") or because we were provoked ("How dare he say that to me!"). Meanwhile, though, we are harsh when others commit the same sin or exhibit the same flaw. This is such a classic foible of humanity that Jesus told a parable about the unmerciful servant who begged the master to relieve him of his debt and, instead of practicing mercy himself, immediately turned around and demanded his fellow servant to pay a much smaller debt at once (Matthew 18:21–35).

Uncovering the False Self

Thomas Merton wrote in his autobiography that the false self was a kind of fallout from original sin. Later on, he wrote this:

Every one of us is shadowed by an illusory person: a false self. ... We are not very good at recognizing illusions, least of all the ones we cherish about ourselves — the ones we are born with and which feed the roots of sin."[5]

All the false personae, the ways we may have developed over the years to cope with a past wound or a dysfunctional childhood, the worldly attachments that we adorn our lives with and use to wield power over others or to gain prestige or control — all these keep us from being authentically loving of God and others. At best, they are like layers of dust and grime that keep us from being able to see out the window of our souls. At worst, they darken our souls through sinful attachments that prevent the love of Christ from dwelling in us.

And, at bottom, it is fear.

It is fear that what we will see there in that bear-infested cabin is so disgusting that we could not continue to live remotely happy lives. It is fear that we are unlovable. It is the fear of being absolutely alone. Pope Benedict XVI said that ultimately all fear is the fear of total abandonment, absolute loneliness. Jesus Christ went down into hell to free us from the total abandonment of death, to bring love to even the depths of hell.[6] There is no darkness so dark that Christ cannot shine his light into it. There is no pit of despair so deep that God's love cannot penetrate it.

Fraternal Correction

The concept of fraternal correction has deep biblical roots. In the Letter to the Hebrews, Saint Paul writes: "My son, do not disdain the discipline of the Lord / or lose heart when reproved by him" (Hebrews 12:5, NABRE). Sometimes, the Lord uses others to help us become aware of the faults we need to correct, and other times he will allow suffering in our life for the same purpose. We need to try to respond gracefully and with peaceful acceptance to the criticism, however it comes. Being open to criticism requires disciplined listening and trust in our interpersonal relationships, through which healing and mercy shine through.

When God Corrects

We also face correction from God himself. One of the results of original sin is that we have a tendency to avoid taking an honest look at ourselves. As soon as Adam had eaten the fruit that Eve gave him, he denied all responsibility and even blamed God: "The woman whom you gave to be with me, she gave me fruit of the tree" (Genesis 3:12). Worse yet, we tend to silence the bearers of truth because we cannot bear to hear it: many of the Old Testament prophets were killed or mistreated. Though Herod was intrigued by what John the Baptist said about marriage, his wife was enraged and had him beheaded. And Jesus Christ — Truth himself — was crucified and suffered an ignominious death on the cross.

By seeking always to know ourselves (and not just superficially) and by practicing the daily regimen of doing a nightly examination of conscience, we can fight against that natural tendency. By going to confession frequently, we work on those sinful habits we would rather not face. Penance helps free us from our attachment to sin and frees us to love more purely. God corrects us in different ways — sometimes through the sufferings he permits us to undergo.

— PRACTICAL APPLICATION —

In this section, we are going to discuss both giving and receiving constructive criticism.

When addressing problems or bringing up a complaint, we recommend using the "softened start-up." When you want to ask your boss for a raise, you increase the likelihood that he will listen to you if you don't pounce on him as you are riding up the elevator to your office. Rather, you would make an appointment with him to discuss something important. Now, he is prepared. The same goes for bringing up a problem or a complaint. If you pounce on the other person as soon as they walk in the door after a long commute ("Why are you late again? You are always late!"), you are likely to create defensiveness and they are less likely to listen. Defensiveness kills communication. Using the softened start-up eases into an issue or invites the other person to discuss the topic at the time of their choosing. It can be soothing, orienting small talk or asking permission to bring up a topic.

Laraine (though she is a choleric who would much prefer getting straight to the point) once used this technique very successfully when she wanted to bring up a problem with Art. After we had agreed to have family dinners on a regular basis, Art suddenly and mysteriously turned into Emily Post. He decided to critique everyone's bad table manners — how they passed the salt or spoke with their mouth still full. This often resulted in hurt feelings, with a child (or Laraine) storming off from the table in a huff. The effect they had hoped for — family congeniality, discussing each child's day, improved communication as a family — resulted in the opposite: frustration, fighting, misunderstandings.

Laraine decided that this was an opportunity to practice her newly learned communication skill, the softened start-up. She began this way, "There's something that has been bothering me lately and I would like to discuss it with you when you have time." Art was naturally intrigued and didn't wait long to discuss it with her. Then, when it was time to bring the problem up, Laraine began with a positive statement, "I really appreciate the way you have been trying to make it home early enough so we can have dinner as a family!" And then she addressed the issue of being overly critical at dinner.

The second skill necessary when bringing up problems or complaints is to express the underlying positive, as Laraine did above. You remind yourself of the good intentions of the other person, and you state them before stating your complaint. As we described earlier, when we bury our feelings or stockpile our grievances, the bad feelings tend to increase until all we see is the negative. This dangerous situation can result in an explosion of negativity or distancing and withdrawing from the relationship. The underlying positive is the antidote to negative-sentiment override.

Instead of "Why can't you ever get it through your head that I hate going over to your mother's house?" try this: "I appreciate that you are dedicated to your mom and want to be with her, but instead of all of us driving over to your mom's house, how about we all meet for breakfast at IHOP?"

When offering constructive criticism, it is best to stick to one topic at a time, to reduce the likelihood of flooding. Also, remember to focus on the particular issue, rather than judging the person or his character: coming home late, not "you are a bad father."

Now, let's move to ways of listening to constructive criticism.

It is always helpful to be aware of how you tend to react, based on your temperament. As we noted earlier, cholerics have a tendency to react swiftly, angrily, and to go immediately on the offensive. And melancholics tend to take the criticism very personally and to brood over it for days. Knowing how we tend to respond helps us prepare for the eventual critical comment. We can resolve to listen attentively (in order to understand) without reacting immediately. And then respond in such a way that you show your partner that you understood what he or she was saying.

Instead of "It's not my fault! I was told by the assistant principal to send that e-mail to the parents!" respond in such a way that the speaker knows we understand: "So you would prefer that I check with you first before sending any e-mails to the parents, is that correct?"

Instead of not responding and sulking in your office when your boss makes a critical comment, try going to him and saying: "I was really taken aback by the comments you made yesterday about my being late for the meeting last Wednesday. Can we discuss why I was late?"

When your spouse says, "You left the milk out on the counter again!" don't reply, "Well I have to balance the checkbook for you!" Try, "I'm sorry; I will try to remember next time."

Exercise

Pick a partner and ask him or her to provide you with some constructive criticism. For example, ask a co-worker to give you feedback on a recent project, or ask your spouse or good friend how you might be able to be a more loving and attentive spouse/friend. Evaluate your own level of defensiveness and capacity to respond with equanimity and grace. You can then trade places and practice the "softened start-up" in order to bring up a difficult topic with your partner, without arousing defensiveness in him or her. Try asking permission to discuss the topic or begin by complimenting your partner on the many ways they grace your life and bring joy to your world.

CHAPTER 5

Listening to Wisdom

Laraine recently stumbled upon an old photo of herself with our favorite professor from our undergraduate years, Father Timothy Fallon, S.J. Laraine is twenty-two, sporting old jeans and a goofy seventies hairdo. Father Fallon is tall, elegant, white-haired, and goateed, looking a lot like Colonel Sanders. Why on earth, we wonder today, did he so generously spend time with us? We were young and foolish; he was wise and patient.

Even before we met as undergraduates at a Jesuit university, we both shared a love for the same philosophy professor, a wisdom figure in that critical time of our lives. He taught many different philosophy courses, but all were taught from the perspective of his own former professor, the great Jesuit theologian, philosopher, and priest Bernard Lonergan. We struggled to keep up with those classes, all the while laughing at Father Fallon's jokes and use of physical comedy to portray key philosophical positions. For example, demonstrating Zeno's paradox by trying, but failing, to walk across the classroom. After graduating, we stayed in touch, dining at the Jesuit residence — which he dubbed the "Home for Unwed

Fathers" — visiting him at the University of Toronto, partici-
pating in the Bernard Lonergan symposia, and simply enjoy-
ing his company. He married us, baptized two of our children,
and baptized the children of our best friends as well.

He was wise in part because he was brilliant in his area
of expertise; but more than that, he was funny, approachable,
accepting, sensitive, and generous. He also had suffered greatly
during his life, and this made him compassionate and even
wiser. He loved teaching, he loved the Lord, and he was a
beautiful soul. Wisdom is more than knowledge.

We all can think of a wise person — someone who greatly
influenced our lives — perhaps a perceptive teacher, a contemplative priest, a sensitive grandparent, a gentle confessor,
an insightful counselor, a demanding coach, a knowledgeable colleague, or another wisdom figure. It is striking that
the best word to describe these sages is "wise." They may be
learned, knowledgeable, sensitive, empathic, enlightened, or
otherwise profoundly adept in their area of expertise, which
may be simply being our parent or grandparent! Yet "wise"
is the one word that actually captures them. We all know
very knowledgeable people whom we would never call wise.
They may know "things," but they do not have that sensitivity to others, that compassion, or that generosity of spirit
that makes them truly wise. A wisdom figure is sensitive and
intuitive, grasps something profound about our souls, shares
their insights with us, and somehow resonates with the core
of our being.

Largeness of Mind

The word "wisdom" appears more than 230 times in the Bible. Certain biblical figures are wise: Solomon, Judith, God himself. There are admonitions about wisdom in Proverbs, prayers for wisdom in the Psalms, musings on the meaning of wisdom in Job and Ecclesiastes, and the identification of Wisdom with God in the Book of Wisdom. Why does this word appear so frequently?

The author of the Book of Wisdom — according to tradition King Solomon — says that he had an abundance of natural gifts, yet he begs God for wisdom: "Now I was a well-favored child, / and I came by a noble nature; / or rather, being noble, I attained an unblemished body" (Wisdom 8:19, NABRE). "Therefore I prayed, and understanding was given me; / I called upon God, and the spirit of wisdom came to me" (Wisdom 7:7). "And God gave Solomon wisdom and understanding beyond measure, and largeness of mind like the sand on the seashore" (1 Kings 4:29).

What a beautiful image: largeness of mind like the sand on a seashore! Visualize standing on the seashore, the sand spreading out to your right and to your left as far as you can see, smooth and untouched except by the vast ocean whose waves lace the shore with frothy foam. This "largeness of mind" is an aspect that we intuitively grasp when we say that someone is "wise." Their understanding is as deep as the ocean and as wide as the sea. They grasp more than the objects of knowledge, and they share that understanding with us.

Wisdom Dwells in Prudence (Proverbs 8:12)

An aspect of wisdom is prudence, which is not only knowing what the good is; it is also choosing the right means to attain it (see the *Catechism of the Catholic Church* 1806). According to Saint Thomas Aquinas, prudence is "right reason in action," correctly applying moral principles to practical situations of our daily life.

There are times in our lives when we are stumped as to what the correct decision might be with regard to a job, our vocation, our marriage, or our children. It is prudent at such times to seek the advice of a trusted friend or a wise counselor and to take it to prayer. We consider it a sign of maturity when our teenage children do not resist the notion of seeking the advice of a teacher or counselor when they are stuck. Prudence requires discernment, intelligent grasping of moral principles, and making reasonable judgments and decisions.

Many years ago, Art was embarking on a new stage in his career as a marriage and family therapist. He would be in charge of counseling programs overseas, working hand in hand with the U.S. military to help dependents who were struggling with substance abuse. We had a three-year-old and a baby and began packing our bags for a great adventure in Europe. Fortunately, Art recognized that working with the military was different than working directly with troubled teens or special-needs kids, as he had done previously. Though he would still be working with clients, his client was also the military. Many other therapists had flamed out in a similar position, for they failed to grasp the command structure of the military. And to add to the challenge, even before beginning this new job, Art had three strikes against him: he was a civilian, he was a contractor, and he was a "flaky" therapist — a profession rarely admired by the military at that time.

But Art had a secret weapon: his father-in-law, a retired Army full colonel, with thirty-three years in the military, a five-time Purple Heart recipient, decorated with the Legion of Merit and many other medals for his decades of service to our country. Bill mentored Art through the military culture, telling him which criticisms to ignore and which to take seriously; how to show respect to officers and enlisted; how to "sell" clinical interventions as advancing the local mission and how to reduce the fear of counseling by calling the sessions "strategy meetings"; and to remind parents that they were the benevolent leaders of their kids. Art was able to succeed where many others did not, and he was even promoted to running the entire program in Europe and eventually Asia. Art was successful because he knew when to seek advice, and he listened to wisdom.

Listen Carefully, Love Deeply

Conversatio morum is an ancient term found in the Rule of Benedict and a vow that Benedictines make in addition to fidelity and obedience. It is commonly understood as fidelity to the monastic way of life. Yet it is actually rather mysterious. Eighth-century monks who were transcribing the

Rule thought that Saint Benedict meant to write *"conversio"* — conversion, meaning conversion of heart. The mistake was discovered a thousand years later, and the original term was restored to the Rule. What did Saint Benedict mean by *conversatio morum*? *Morum*: habit, will, way; *conversatio* meant frequent abode in a place, conversation. Scholars suggest that the way Saint Benedict used it implies that he meant a commitment to the monastic life. It also encompasses "conversion" in that the monastic way is always turning toward God, seeking to do his will, and turning away from sin.

Judith Valente, author of *Atchison Blue: A Search for Silence, a Spiritual Home, and a Living Faith*, writes that a Benedictine nun explained *conversatio morum* in this way: "It's a call to listen carefully, to love deeply, and to be willing to change as needed."[1]

Valente tells of her struggle to incorporate *conversatio morum* into her daily life. One Christmas she was cranky and ungrateful about some gifts she had received from her stepdaughters — despite having vowed to work on her difficult relationship with them for the sake of her husband. Also, despite having been on retreat with the Benedictines, where she had resolved to practice *conversatio* — conversion — in her daily life. Frustrated with herself, she sought spiritual advice from wise elderly Sister Thomasita. Sister later sent her an email, recommending that she slowly read 1 Corinthians 13 ("Love is patient, love is kind ..."), and a second time slowly, substituting "God" for "Love," and yet again a third time, substituting her own name.

This was wise advice from a trusted friend and spiritual leader in her life. Yet we do not always turn readily to wisdom to seek advice when we are struggling with life. How often do we really attend to a Sunday homily and take it to heart? Or consult with a professional counselor? Or study some of the great spiritual writers available to us as Catholics? Or turn to an elderly grandparent, whose years on earth have earned the status of wisdom? There are so many sources of wisdom, yet pride and vanity — and sometimes laziness! — prevent us from asking their advice. It takes humility to admit that we do not have all the answers and to seek counsel — whether in psychological, spiritual, or professional matters. Yet so often, we are like the fool in Proverbs: "The fear of the LORD is the beginning of knowledge; / fools despise wisdom and instruction" (Proverbs 1:7).

Art had a client once who was highly intelligent, successful, and accomplished in many areas. But things started to go awry. His daughter became ill, his communication with his wife deteriorated, and he felt himself growing distant from her. He began to struggle at work but had no mentor or colleague with whom to discuss his problems. He became more and more isolated, distancing himself even from the sacraments. He eventually began seeing another woman. His wife found out, and his life and family unraveled completely. Fortunately, his wife demanded that he go to marriage counseling with her. This finally broke the spell of the isolation that had robbed him of all faith that anyone — whether God or another person — could reach into that darkness and pull him out.

The Wisdom of the Desert

In the fourth century A.D., a large movement began in the deserts of Egypt, Arabia, Syria, and Palestine. Men and women went to live as hermits in the desert, in great austerity and poverty, seeking the will of God and to live fully the Gospel message.

These simple men and women — seeking God with all their heart, soul, mind, and strength (cf. Mark 12:30) — became known for their wisdom. And many people came from the cities and countryside to ask their advice. They were, essentially, the first spiritual directors. We call them the Desert Fathers and Mothers, and their collections of wise sayings and paradoxical, sometimes humorous stories are occasionally reminiscent of Zen koans. Many of their "lessons" point to the virtue of humility, the importance of not judging one's neighbor, and seeking God with a pure heart.

For example, here are two stories that Thomas Merton shared, the first one about wise Abbot Anthony, who wished to test some of his fellow monks on their understanding of various scriptural passages. After he had quizzed them on a particular text and the monks had responded with their best interpretations, he turned to Abbot Joseph:

> What about you? What do you say this text means? Abbot Joseph replied: I know not! Then Abbot Anthony said: Truly Abbot Joseph alone has found the way, for he replies that he knows not....[2]

In the second story, "Abbot Joseph asked Abbot Pastor: Tell me how I can become a monk. The elder replied: If you want to have rest here in this life and also in the next, in every conflict with another say: Who am I? And judge no one."[3]

During our pilgrimage to the Holy Land, we were struck by the actual desert there — not the lovely azure skies and soft sage colors of the New Mexican desert, but the harsh, rock-strewn, and cave-ridden mountains of the Middle East. Jutting high above the palm tree-lined city of Jericho is the Mount of Temptation, where Satan tempted Jesus after he had fasted and prayed for forty days. Perilously balanced on the side of the mountain in the craggy rocks is a monastery. There the monks pray in silence, high above the world with all its riches and temptations, the endless blue of the sky meeting the harsh and barren mountain. Surely these monks gain a wisdom not found readily in the world.

Wisdom of the World vs. Wisdom of the Just

One of the most dramatic and challenging books of the Old Testament is the Book of Job. Theologians, philosophers, priests, and Talmudic and literary scholars alike have weighed in on this story of one man's struggle to understand his plight and to remain faithful to God throughout his afflictions. Job is a truly good and pious man, who offers daily sacrifices in reparation for any *potential* sins of his children. The devil challenges God to test the "blameless and upright" man. He reminds God, "Have you not surrounded him and his family and all that he has with your protection? ... But now put forth your hand and touch all that he has, and surely he will curse you to your face" (Job 1:10, 11, NABRE). God allows Satan to destroy everything that Job has, kill his ten children, and afflict him with a terrible illness. All Job's friends turn against him. They assume he must have done something wrong to have brought this suffering upon him and his family. The ultimate question is really the problem of evil: Why does God allow the innocent to suffer? Job himself, in an attempt to explain to his supposedly wise friends what is happening, says, "With God are wisdom and might; / he has counsel and understanding" (Job 12:13).

Job does not understand God's purpose, but as God reminds him toward the end of the book, he shouldn't expect to. The Lord finally speaks to him, his voice booming out of the whirlwind: "Where were you when I laid the foundation of the earth?" (Job 38:4). (Essentially: *I am God, and you cannot comprehend me.*) Finally, Job repents in dust and ashes (Job 42:6). Job's humility allows him to believe in God even when his world is falling apart: *God is God, and I am not.* Such humility allows us to be receptive disciples.

Pope Saint Gregory the Great says that Job had the wisdom of the just — despite having been mocked and thought to be a fool. His innocence was considered foolishness by the world. This is reminiscent of Saint Paul to the Corinthians: "For the foolishness of God is wiser than men, and the weakness of God is stronger than men" (1 Corinthians 1:25).

Job had the wisdom of the just, as opposed to the wisdom of the world. The wisdom of the world is to conceal one's thoughts — at best, to be astute and politic; at worst, cunning and deceitful, making "what is false appear true and what is true appear false."[4] The wisdom of the just, in contrast, is "never to pretend anything for show," but to speak the truth, "to do what is right without reward and to be more willing to put up with evil than to perpetrate it, not to seek revenge for wrong...."[5]

The knowledge of the wise is on a transcendent level. They seem to dwell in the "thin spaces," those spaces where heaven seems to meet the earth. Sometimes attributed to the Celts or to pre-Christian Irish, these were places on earth that held spiritual power. When you are standing in a cathedral where the arches seem to lift straight to heaven, or you glimpse the sun just rising above the mountains, casting a glow over the earth, or you are overwhelmed by the vast multitude of stars over a midnight ocean — these are thin spaces.

The wise person is so because "the LORD gives wisdom" (Proverbs 2:6), and the one who is wisdom itself is God. As Father John Hardon said, "The Real Presence is the manifestation of the wisdom of God. The theme of St. John's Gospel is that the Word of God, which is the wisdom of God, became flesh and dwelt among us. St. Paul told the Corinthians, 'Christ [is] the wisdom of God' (1 Corinthians 1:24)."[6]

Only as we grow closer to Christ and learn to see things from his perspective do we grow in wisdom ourselves. It is a gift of the Holy Spirit. This is not wisdom in the natural sense but rather in the supernatural order. It makes our soul responsive to the Holy Spirit in the contemplation of divine things and allows us to think "with the mind of Christ" (1 Corinthians 2:16). This gift of the Holy Spirit is conferred on us at Confirmation. We pray for a fresh outpouring of the Holy Spirit and pray that the gifts of the Holy Spirit be renewed and stirred up within each of us.

Pope Francis picked up the same thread when, in his morning meditation, he discussed how the spirit of wisdom triumphs over worldly curiosity. Holiness, he explained, is a matter of "coming under the influence and movement of God's Spirit and of this wisdom."[7] This wisdom is "intelligent, holy, unique, / Manifold, subtle, agile, / clear, unstained, certain, / Never harmful, loving the good, keen…" (Wisdom 7:22, NABRE). Again, Pope Francis: "Let us allow the Spirit to lead us forward with the wisdom of a soft breeze. This is the spirit of the kingdom of God of which Jesus speaks."[8]

Wisdom as Divine Contemplation

The author of the Book of Ecclesiastes writes, "I said, 'I will acquire wisdom'; but it was far beyond me. What exists is far-reaching; it is deep, very deep: Who can find it out?" (Ecclesiastes 7:23–24, NABRE).

When we find someone who is wise, we recognize — if only nascently — an element of divinity. No human being can be perfectly wise, as that is reserved for God himself. Yet we may catch a glimpse of it — and if we are humble and our hearts are open, we will seek that person's advice. Wisdom includes an element of love. "This is what wisdom does," says

Father Hardon. "It gives us the capacity to enjoy what we believe and to find deep satisfaction in reflecting on the truth that we possess."[9]

Laraine once consulted her spiritual director about the longing she had to live in the country. "I want to have chickens and goats and have a view of the mountains from my back porch." He listened patiently and attentively (with only a twinkle in his eye) and then, as I waited to hear his profound advice, he laughed heartily and said, "Laraine, you would go crazy within two weeks!" This is the sort of knowledge — mingled with loving friendship — that is instantly recognizable as wisdom.

But this contemplation inspired by love reaches its fulfillment in the knowledge and understanding of divine things, the contemplation of God and his truth.

Saint Columban was a sixth-century Irish missionary who founded monasteries in what is now France and Italy. In his instructions to his monks, he reflected on the depths of God in a way that is reminiscent of the author of the Book of Ecclesiastes' "deep, very deep": "God is everywhere in his immensity, and everywhere close at hand." Yet instead of despairing of ever finding wisdom, he concluded with this advice: "Seek then the highest wisdom, not by arguments in words but by the perfection of your life."[10]

And so, we might say that our life itself, our actions, will reflect whether we have become wise.

Consider the biblical heroine Abigail, the beautiful and wise wife of the crude, ill-tempered Nabal (see 1 Samuel 25).

She saved her household from destruction by quickly and prudently apologizing for her husband's rude ingratitude toward David and by making reparation for Nabal's insult. Her wise action was both "moral and messianic" in that she both saved her family and furthered God's divine purpose.[11] This story hints at the supernatural aspect of true wisdom: it works not only for the good, humanly speaking, but also it furthers God's salvific plan.

Or consider Judith, a God-fearing, prayerful widow, who dared to speak up to the elders and challenge their plan to surrender to the Assyrians: "Who are you, that have put God to the test this day...?" (Judith 8:12).

The wisdom of God is a mystery, Saint Paul tells us (1 Corinthians 2:7), and "a breath of the power of God" (Wisdom 7:25) — yet God reveals himself to us through his Son:

For while gentle silence enveloped all things,
and night in its swift course was now half gone,
your all-powerful word leaped from heaven,
    from the royal throne,
into the midst of the land that was doomed...."
(Wisdom 18:14-15)

— PRACTICAL APPLICATION —

Take a moment to pray in silence for the gift of wisdom. Ask God to stir up in your soul the gifts you received at Confirmation.

Pope Saint John Paul II prayed to the Holy Spirit every day from the time he was a young child. Following his example, pray this prayer to the Holy Spirit:

> Come, Holy Spirit, fill the hearts of your faithful and kindle in them the fire of your love. Send forth your Spirit and they shall be created. And you shall renew the face of the earth.
>
> O, God, who by the light of the Holy Spirit, did instruct the hearts of the faithful, grant that by the same Holy Spirit we may be truly wise and ever enjoy his consolations, through Christ Our Lord. Amen.

Exercise

Write down the names of some people whose wisdom you are grateful for. Write them a note or a letter, thanking them for their wisdom or guidance over the years. Research has shown that people who write letters of gratitude are happier following this exercise than before. If your mentors have passed away, consider having a Mass said for the repose of their souls.

Perhaps you have some unresolved questions in your life — whether about your job, relationships, or spiritual life; write these down, too. Is there a wise person you might consult in regard to this issue? Leave this blank, if you do not know someone, or fill in a name. Just making this list will keep the notion fresh in your mind, and it will not be long before someone's name will appear on the horizon and you will know that is the person to contact.

Art's knee had been deteriorating steadily despite taking nutritional supplements and refraining from running. Even walking was becoming nearly impossible. When he was unable to even walk the dog farther than a block, we knew we had to take action — but Laraine remembered the caution of her good friend who was a nurse, not to go to just any orthopedic surgeon. So we were on the alert when we were giving a talk at a homeschooling group and two of the dads mentioned that they had recently undergone surgery — both for hips. Their surgeon was renowned throughout the area, having treated Washington, D.C., sports teams' injuries and other famous athletes. Moreover, the doctor's son and their family were in our parish! This was just the wisdom we were waiting for, and Art made the appointment the next day. This surgeon was many miles away, yet we knew we had received the best advice.

CHAPTER 6

Listening to God

In the Beginning, God Spoke

Our God, the creator of the universe, is a God who reveals himself in many ways: through the prophets; through Scripture; through Jesus, the Word made flesh; through the Church; through creation itself; and in our souls.

But in the very beginning, he spoke.

The very first words of Scripture tell us that God spoke the universe into existence. When there was nothing but a vast, formless void, God said: "Let there be light" (Genesis 1:3). The nothingness that became the universe listened to the word of God and took light and shape. God speaks, and the universe listens.

He spoke with Adam and Eve in the garden, to Noah and to Abram, with whom he made a covenant. He walked with Abraham in deep conversation, as Abraham pleaded on behalf of any righteous men who might have lived in Sodom and Gomorrah (Genesis 18:22–33). This critical event is a turning point in man's relationship with God. Why is Abraham considered "our father in faith,"[1] and not Noah?

Noah was the only righteous man on earth, and he listened and obeyed. But Abraham interceded with God on behalf of men. He dared even to press the Lord, arguing on behalf of any righteous men who lived in the wicked, doomed city. This event is an example of intercessory prayer. It shows that God wants to be in a relationship with each one of us. He doesn't merely command and we obey, as he did with Noah. God also listens.

> I love the LORD, who listened
> to my voice in supplication,
> Who turned an ear to me
> on the day I called.
> (Psalm 116:1–2, NABRE)

How the Prophets Listened

God spoke to Isaac, Rebekah, Jacob, Job … and to the prophets. Jonah tried to run away from the word of God that had come to him, but in the end he did as the Lord had instructed him.

The prophet Habakkuk tells how he waited to hear God's word: "I will take my stand to watch, / and station myself on the tower, / and look forth to see what he will say to me" (Habakkuk 2:1).

Saint Bernard explains in a sermon that Habakkuk, though expecting reprimands from the Lord (and, indeed, receiving serious threats against the wicked Chaldeans), did not hide from God's words. Rather, he "dwells on them with attentive and anxious care."[2]

Another prophet, Elijah, having just laid to waste the false god Baal and all the false prophets, falls into a depression because Jezebel has sworn to kill him, and because the Israelites have forsaken the covenant with God. In the midst of this depression and desperation, Elijah flees to the mountain — the same mountain where Moses experienced God calling to him out of the burning bush. It is here that one of the most iconic representations of listening to God occurs. On Mount Horeb, Elijah waits for the Lord to pass by. First there is a violent wind, followed by an earthquake and a fire. The Lord is not in any of these dramatic events; instead, Elijah recognizes him in a "still small voice" (1 Kings 19:12).

From the example of Habakkuk and Elijah, we learn that in order to hear the word of God one must "keep watch" — as Jesus also told his followers during the agony in the garden — and *listen* for a small, quiet, and ultimately mysterious voice.

As Pope Benedict XVI said, "Becoming silent means discovering a new order of things. ... Silence means developing the inner senses ... the sensitivity to the eternal in us, the ability to listen to God."[3] God made us in his image and likeness. God is a communion of persons, a God of relationships, of intimacy, of love. Thomas Merton once said that when we listen to God, we are hearing a loving conversation among the three Persons of the Blessed Trinity.[4] "What I say, therefore, I say as the Father has bidden me" (John 12:50).

God Speaks to Us in Different Ways

He speaks to us through Scripture, through the Church, through circumstances, through creation, and especially to our hearts in prayer.

When we read Scripture, we are reading something that is unlike any other written work. We are reading the divinely inspired words of God that are living and true, speaking to us in the very moment we read them. God's word is eternal, and he speaks to each one of us personally. The *Catechism* tells us that Christ, through the Holy Spirit, will "open [our] minds to understand the Scriptures" (CCC 108), just as he did to the disciples on the road to Emmaus.

When Christ introduces the Great Commandment in the Gospel of Mark, he is telling us to listen: "Hear, O Israel: The Lord our God, the Lord is one" (12:29). "Hear, O Israel ..." (known as the *Shema*) is so important to the Jewish people that they recite this Scripture daily, morning and evening, and these are their last words on earth.

So important is listening that we must, said Benedict XVI, *begin* as a listening person: "before doing comes hearing."[5]

This doesn't mean that we can interpret God's words in Scripture any way we want to; for that, we should take Holy Mother Church as our guide. We should be attentive "*to the content and unity of the whole Scripture*" and read Scripture within the "*living Tradition of the whole Church,*" "*attentive to the analogy of faith*" (CCC 112, 113, 114, emphasis in original). With these three guideposts in mind, we will not inadvertently misunderstand what God is saying to us as we read Sacred Scripture.

Using the Guideposts

A very real example of how we should use the guideposts to inform us as we interpret Scripture is the sad (and true) story of a young woman, Candace, who was a practicing Catholic, wife, and mother to four young children.[6] She struck up a friendship with one of her children's teachers. This young woman was carefree, fun-loving, and charismatic, and the two bonded over the young teacher's remarkable ability to entertain and bring the best out of Candace's kindergartener. The young teacher, however, was an active lesbian. The young Catholic mom was fascinated and allured, and because she was having marital difficulties with her husband, she began to think about leaving. She turned to Scripture and found, "Whoever is without love does not know God, for God is love" (1 John 4:8, NABRE). She couldn't find anything saying that she wasn't allowed to follow her bliss in this new way. Her mistake, of course, was that she didn't consider the teachings of the Church.

Listening to God in Creation

Sarah Salviander is a research scientist with a Ph.D. in astrophysics who, for most of her life, was an atheist. It wasn't until she was a in her mid-twenties that she began to question her atheism. As she studied deuterium abundances in the universe in support of the Big Bang theory, she realized that every question seems to have an answer. She writes, "There's no reason it has to be this way, and it made me think of Einstein's observation that the most incomprehensible thing about the world is that it's comprehensible. I started to sense an underlying order to the universe."[7]

There are many stories about atheist scientists who have become believers in God through their scientific research — often through their study of cosmology or through study of molecular biology. The elegance of the universe, the intelligibility and coherence of everything, from the Big Bang to DNA, speaks to the existence of a God who designed the universe.

Other ex-atheists describe their conversion through the beauty and wonder of creation. One man undertook a sailing trip to unpopulated regions. Out in his boat under the vast expanse of the midnight sky where no artificial light interfered with his view of the hundreds of millions of stars overhead, this man slowly realized there must be a God.

As the psalmist writes, "The heavens are telling the glory of God; / and the firmament proclaims his handiwork" (Psalm 19:1) The beauty of nature draws our hearts and minds to God. The universe with its fearsome magnitude came into existence at God's word and at every moment speaks to us. Our breath is taken away when we are surrounded by the awesome majesty of snow-topped mountains or the vast expanse of millions of stars overhead as we sail across the water.

We can be surprised by the marvels and beauty of creation as we take a walk close to home. We recall one spring day when a chorus of spring peepers surprised us as we hiked through the fields of the Manassas battlefield in Virginia. It is no wonder that God chose an astronomical event, the star of Bethlehem, to draw the Magi to the birthplace of his Son. And we are told to read the "signs of the times" in nature when the second coming draws near:

> "From the fig tree learn its lesson: as soon as its branch becomes tender and puts forth its leaves, you know that summer is near. So also, when you see all these things, you know that he is near, at the very gates." (Matthew 24:32–33)

Calming the Anxiety of Life

Doesn't it often happen that we get so caught up in the busyness of our lives that we forget to begin and end each day with prayer? All it takes is a simple prayer of thanksgiving for being alive and having another chance to "do something beautiful for God," as Mother Teresa used to say. But our lives can get so hectic that as soon as our feet hit the floor we are off and running.

Then something will happen that sends us to our knees. Whether it's anxiety about finances, distress about a loved one, a serious illness, or hearing about a friend who passed away, now prayer time becomes urgent.

These motivations may not be the most supernatural or laudable, but they are very human. Yet even our first impulse to pray is a gift. We enter into prayer through the "narrow gate of *faith*" (CCC 2656, emphasis in original). Faith itself is a theological virtue, a gift from God. Whether we turn to God in moments of distress or whether we turn to him daily out of love, we can do so only because he has called us first and has given us the gift of faith.

It may begin with anxiety about our life, stress due to work, fears about love and death, desire for happiness, or whatever else. But as Pope Benedict (when he was Cardinal Ratzinger) said, we can try to distract ourselves by throwing ourselves into our work or else we can "carry around in ourselves all that oppresses us." Better, he added, we can convert all these fears, longings, hopes, and anxieties into prayer:

> A single hour of quiet listening to the word of God would often be more effective than whole stacks of paper, for it is not only what we do that makes us effective. Sometimes the impression arises that behind our hectic hyperactivity there lurks a paralysis of faith ... we become mature and free and genuine by sinking the roots of our being into the fruitful stillness of God."[8]

When we lift our hearts and minds to God, we begin to find the peace we are longing for. It allows us to overcome our own selfishness and competitive spirit to become open to loving encounters with others.

Listening Through Prayer

A visiting priest from a neighboring parish preached a powerful homily one Sunday on the parable of the Good Samaritan. He made this parable come alive by relating a personal experience. He was headed to the Dominican House of Studies in Washington, D.C., to speak with his spiritual director.

He arrived at the massive Gothic structure and noted that, of the two paths he could take to the front door, one — the shortest path — was occupied by a skinny African American man holding a paper bag, shuffling toward him. He thought to himself, "This homeless guy is probably going to hit me up for a handout."

So he took the other path, which led all the way around the back of the building and finally deposited him at the front door. He rang the doorbell. Nobody answered. He rang it again. Nobody answered. He rang it a third time.

And then he felt the presence of someone standing next to him. He knew it was Jesus. Father says sheepishly, "That homeless guy was you, wasn't it?" And Jesus replied, "Yes, it was. Now go and talk to him." So Father went all the way back around to the other path and struck up a conversation. The man showed him the contents of his bag — medicine and syringes, diabetic paraphernalia — and he explained that he had been diagnosed with diabetes and asked the priest to pray for him. Father assured him of his prayers. And just as they were saying good-bye, the man asked if the priest could spare twenty dollars.

This got a big laugh. But the parallel to the priest in the Gospel of Luke crossing the road to avoid the man beaten by robbers and left for dead was compelling (Luke 10:31). Jesus does not often speak to us so dramatically. More often this interior voice is the fruit of our own prayer and constant communication with God.

More significantly, God is drawing our attention to the fact that he is always present in the ordinary circumstances of our lives. He was there in the homeless man carrying a bag of syringes. He speaks to us through the ordinary.

What We Learn from Naaman the Leper

Naaman was the commander of the Syrian army and held in high esteem by the king. "He was a mighty man of valor, but he was a leper" (2 Kings 5:1). Naaman went to Israel in search of a cure, having heard from a maid that there was a prophet there who could heal him. When Elisha the prophet told him to wash seven times in the Jordan, he was insulted and angry.

Was that all this so-called prophet could come up with? Why, there were better rivers in Syria! No dramatic display, no fanfare? Naaman was about to leave in disgust when his servants pleaded with him to do what the prophet said. They appealed to his reason: "If the prophet had commanded you to do some great thing, would you not have done it?" (2 Kings 5:13). So Naaman washed in the Jordan and was cured. So often we, too, think that God should speak to us in some spectacular way. We think we should hear his voice clearly, receive a dramatic sign, or experience overwhelming consolations of peace and joy when we pray. We bemoan the dullness of the liturgy or we rail at God when we experience setbacks and trials in our lives. Yet all this ordinary stuff is the means God uses to speak to us!

As Father Kilian Healy, O.Carm., says,

He is to be found in common, ordinary things. When God became man, He chose for His mother a quiet, unknown woman. His birthplace was not a palace, but a cave. During His life, He walked and talked with ordinary people. He chose fishermen as His companions. He did not dine with Herod, but in the homes of common people. He was crucified between two common thieves. He can be found where the unspiritual least expect to find him — in common things.[9]

The alienated protagonist of Walker Percy's novel *The Moviegoer*, Binx Bolling, is an aimless stockbroker living in New Orleans who finds pleasure in movies and women. But he enters on an existential search that brings him to love and the glimmering of faith. He asks himself when he sees a man coming out of a Catholic church on Ash Wednesday, "[I]s it because he believes that God himself is present here at the corner of Elysian Fields and Bons Enfants?"

We need to become more sensitive and alert to the subtle ways God presents himself. We can cultivate that interior awareness or sensitivity that alerts us to God's presence and how he is speaking to us in our daily lives. If we are constantly immersed in the distractions of our daily lives, our "God-sense" may become dulled from disuse. And we will fail to set aside the necessary time to develop the silence and interior space within which we can listen to God. We need to set aside time for quiet prayer.

But We Are So Busy!

How can we set aside time for prayer with the hectic lives we lead? Can't we simply *pray always* (1 Thessalonians 5:17)? We can always offer everything up as a prayer — doing the dishes or caring for a sick child or commuting, enduring the daily trials of life. But this is not enough. The *Catechism* tells us, "We cannot pray 'at all times' if we do not pray at specific times" (CCC 2697).

Why is this?

It's a little like saying that you don't have to say "I love you" to your spouse because *of course* he or she knows this; after all, he works hard to support the family and keeps the lawn mowed. She works and takes the kids to their doctor's appointments. Certainly acts of service convey our love to the other. But we need to hear the words "I love you" as well. And we need to have deep, intimate moments when we pour out our hearts to each other. We need to be fully *present* to each other, and not just doing our daily chores.

Saint Teresa of Ávila famously said that prayer is nothing more than speaking with one whom you love. If that is so, why would we not do this daily?

According to the *Catechism*, "prayer is the living relationship of the children of God with their Father who is good beyond measure, with his Son Jesus Christ and with the Holy Spirit. ... [T]he life of prayer is the habit of being in the presence of the thrice-holy God and in communion with him" (CCC 2565). And God himself calls us to an encounter with him.

Mary of Bethany sat at the Lord's feet, *listening*.

We have heard the Scripture passage about Martha and Mary so many times that we sometimes are tempted to gloss over it: Yeah, yeah, Martha was busy, and Mary had the better part. And that better part, we assume is prayer. But the text says that Mary was just listening to the Lord (Luke 10:39).

The key point is that listening to Jesus is the most important thing. Whether we are active or praying, we must always listen to God. As Pope Francis puts it so succinctly in a homily:

A guest must be listened to. Certainly, the answer Jesus gives Martha — when he tells her that only one thing is necessary — finds its full meaning in reference to hearing the word of Jesus himself, this word that enlightens and sustains all that we are and all that we do. If we are going to pray, for example, before a crucifix, and we talk and talk and talk and then we leave, we don't listen to Jesus. We don't allow him to speak to our hearts.

To listen — this word is key. Don't forget it. We can't forget that the word of Jesus enlightens us; it sustains us and sustains all that we are and do.[10]

As the *Catechism* says, "[I]t is the Face of the Lord that we seek and desire; it is his Word that we want to hear and keep.... [I]t is in the present that we encounter him...: 'O that *today* you would hearken to his voice! Harden not your hearts' " (CCC 2656, 2659, emphasis in original). Prayer is a mystery, not merely a mental exercise (an effort of concentration) or a physical one (going to church or maintaining a certain posture). It is not something that is done by our own effort — the Holy Spirit himself aids us and intercedes for us. "Likewise the Spirit helps us in our weakness; for we do not know how to pray as we ought, but the Spirit himself intercedes for us with sighs too deep for words" (Romans 8:26).

How Do We Know It Is God Speaking?

Yet, we often feel puzzled when we do not "hear" the voice of God speaking to our hearts or experience any palpable communication. How do we know that we are not simply hearing our own thoughts? Saints and spiritual writers have some suggestions in this regard. First, God will never tell us something that would contradict his word in Scripture or the teachings of the Church.

Art once had a client come to him in counseling who claimed that God was telling him that, since he no longer loved his wife of twenty-five years, he ought to divorce her and marry his girlfriend. After all, God wants him to "be happy," he said. Art agreed that God wants him to be happy, but it can't be God's voice telling him to break his commandments by running off with his girlfriend! Since this was not the voice of God, Art explored with him why he was unhappy in his marriage.

When we are unsure about whether we are hearing God's voice about important matters, we would be wise to consult a trusted spiritual adviser, our pastor, or a qualified Catholic therapist. Being able to accept direction is a sign of humility and prudence. We may not always be in agreement with such advice. But if we accept the wisdom of others, we may ultimately find ourselves making the prudential decision.

Sometimes we become overly concerned that we are not being obedient to God's will, and we are almost paralyzed by our indecision. God is not trying to trick us by being darkly obscure, waiting for us to misunderstand so that he can pounce on us: "Gotcha! You made the wrong move! You lose!" This is not God's way. He is, rather, the patient father of the prodigal son, lovingly awaiting our return.

Renowned spiritual director Father Jacques Philippe tells us that we should always ask, "What is the Lord's will?" when facing any specific situation. But we will not always get an immediate response! "Sometimes, He simply leaves us free and sometimes, for reasons of His own, He does not manifest Himself."[11] And this is completely normal. Sometimes we torment ourselves trying to discern God's will when God may simply want us to move forward in uncertainty, intending to do good. Father points out that there is a bit of pride involved in always wanting to be 100 percent certain of God's will.

But What if We Don't Hear God at All?

There are times, though, when we feel that we are really trying to listen and we hear nothing. We pray and pray and nothing changes in our lives. Or we have a fervent request that goes unanswered. Saint Monica must have felt just this way, as she prayed day and night — for thirty years! — for her wayward, pagan son.

We all know the end of the story, with her son becoming a bishop and eventually Saint Augustine. So we may not fully appreciate her deep anguish during those years when God seemed not to be listening to her prayers. She would throw herself upon unsuspecting priests, weeping and requesting their prayers as well. Saint Ambrose commented, "Surely the son of so many tears will not perish."

Saint Teresa of Calcutta experienced a dark night that lasted nearly fifty years — nearly her entire life of ministry. She had a mystical experience in 1946, the "call within the call" to serve Jesus in the poorest of the poor that inspired her to found the Sisters of Charity. But after that vision, there was nothing. In fact, it was worse than nothing; she felt "untold darkness," "nothing but emptiness." "He does not want me — He is not there ... the torture and pain I can't explain."[12]

Saint Teresa's dark night seems to have surpassed in length and intensity those described by John of the Cross and Teresa of Ávila: for in both of their descriptions of the various stages that souls may pass through, there was a certainty of God's presence and the eventual cessation of the dark night or period of purification.

After having been liberated from slavery in Egypt, the Israelites wandered forty years in the desert. Can you imagine forty years of not knowing where your home would be or whether you were truly on the right track? But they hadn't been two months out of being forced to make bricks in Egypt, not two months since they had witnessed the miraculous parting of the Red Sea, and they began to grumble against God:

> "Would that we had died by the hand of the LORD in the land of Egypt, when we sat by the fleshpots and ate bread to the full; for you have brought us out into this wilderness to kill this whole assembly with hunger." (Exodus 16:3)

So God in his mercy gave them bread from heaven. "What is it?" they asked, uncomprehending. Soon, they tired even of the bread from heaven and wished they were back in Egypt — slaves, but well fed:

> "O that we had meat to eat! We remember the fish we ate in Egypt for nothing, the cucumbers, the mel-

ons, the leeks, the onions, and the garlic; but now our strength is dried up, and there is nothing at all but this manna to look at." (Numbers 11:4–6)

Spiritual authors have compared dryness in prayer to the experience of Israel in the desert. "There is indeed a very close parallel between the progress of the soul when this paralysis in prayer has become a permanent condition and the wanderings of the Israelites in the desert."[13] When it takes all your grit to bring yourself to a quiet moment with the Lord, you may be tempted to question whether you are on the right path. Like the Israelites, you may long for earlier days, when you were fed with the consolations of God's clear presence. Yet our relationship with God, until we see him face-to-face, must be one of faith and not one of consolation. As Saint Paul tells the Corinthians, "For now we see in a mirror dimly, but then face to face" (1 Corinthians 13:12).

We all have had times in our lives when we seem to be walking through a patch of spiritual desert. Recently, our youngest grandchild underwent his second open-heart surgery at around fifteen months of age. The surgeon was confident that all had been completely fixed and that our grandson would need no further surgeries until he was a teen. Ten days following the surgery, everything fell apart. Our grandson had to be readmitted to intensive care, requiring a feeding tube and oxygen 24/7. One of his lungs appeared to have detached from the heart, so his parents had to carry around an oxygen tank everywhere he went. He had no interest in crawling or eating. He struggled for every breath, he could barely play, and he threw up every day due to the increased medications. The surgeon said there was nothing more he could do and that our grandson's life expectancy was now greatly reduced.

It seemed that all was hopeless. So many prayers had been offered; it seemed that all of Facebook had been praying for Micah. Entire religious communities, even the bishop, were praying. How had it gone so wrong?

Wait for it.

Then, something clearly providential occurred. In seeking a second opinion, Micah was referred to the top surgeon in the country for his particular congenital defect — the very man who pioneered a unique procedure to repair the heart. He conducted a fourteen-hour, open-heart surgery to make a complete repair of Micah's condition. Where there had been no hope, now there is life.

Why does it seem that sometimes we feel confident and filled with the love of God, but at other times everything seems hopeless and we question where God is in all of this?

God Travels to a Distant Country

The entire salvation story rests on a critical incident: the fact that God is absent for a while, during which time human beings unleash all sorts of evil; God warns us through the prophets, and when the prophets are ignored or killed, he sends his own Son, who is also killed. This is the story of the scapegoat — the innocent one who is killed in place of those who deserve it. In this case, it is God himself who sends himself to make right the injustice to God.

In Matthew (21:33–41), Jesus tells the parable of the wicked tenants. "There was a householder who planted a vineyard, and set a hedge around it, and dug a wine press in it, and built a tower, and leased it to tenants, and went into another country" (21:33).

Why does God, who was so active during the creation and involved with Adam and Eve, then leave us on our own, which allows so many to fall into disbelief? Why does the householder — who is in fact the creator of the universe — so innocently assume that he can send his only son and that the tenants will listen to him? Why did he leave us alone in the first place? Why does God go into another country?

This question has been pondered by Talmudic scholars and Christian spiritual authors alike. Erasmo Leiva-Merikakis takes on the question, first drawing our attention to the Hassidic answer that "God *must* be absent for man's sake … if man is ever to grow fully into his divine vocation of becoming the eyes and hands and Heart of God in this world…."[14] God's absence to our senses demands our *listening* continually to his words — not only in Scripture but also in the way we, too, must carry out his work. For the Jews, God's absence is painfully extended, and yet they continue to hope in his return. We realize as Christians that the parable was fulfilled in Christ's passion and death on the cross, and his saving mercy and love encompasses all, even those who would crucify him. Yet Christ departed again; in fact, he must leave us, as he explained: "You heard me say to you, 'I go away, and I will come to you.' If you loved me, you would have rejoiced, because I go to the Father" (John 14:28). Why, then, his further absence?

Leiva-Merikakis explains this "mystical necessity": "When people look for God in a visible form, they will see only each other. When they look for Christ, they will see only Christians."[15] It is so that we will become the Body of Christ. Christ in his human nature must ascend to the Father where he brings with him our humanity, now reconciled with God. With the coming of the Holy Spirit, we are now joined together in the Mystical Body of Christ. We are now true brothers and sisters in Christ, part of the family of God.

This is reminiscent of the poetic words attributed to Saint Teresa of Ávila: "Christ has no body but yours, / No hands, no feet on earth but yours." God's absence allows for his return into our hearts so that we can become his loving presence to one another.

— PRACTICAL APPLICATION —

Set aside fifteen minutes to practice a simple form of meditation, which the *Catechism* recommends in order to deepen our faith and strengthen our will to follow Christ (CCC 2705–2708). Find a place and time when you can be alone, quiet, with no interruptions. For example, first thing in the morning before you begin your busy day. If you need a little motivation, bring your first cup of coffee out onto your porch or patio, where you can hear the robins and watch the sun spread its warm glow over the horizon. But don't get distracted by the ambiance.

Begin by placing yourself in the presence of God, just as Saint Teresa of Ávila recommended. Realize that God is within you. He speaks to your mind and heart, if you will listen. Quieting our restless minds and bodies is key: "Be still, and know that I am God" (Psalm 46:10).

Choose a small passage of Scripture or other spiritual reading. Begin to read slowly. Note if anything stands out to you, as though a flashlight is streaming upon this particular line or sentence. This may be what God wants you to consider in more depth. You may ponder the meaning of a particular passage of Scripture or you may use your imagination, placing yourself in a Gospel scene. Imagine what it must have been like to be in the crowd at the bustling fishing village of Capernaum on the shore of the Sea of Galilee when, in a single day, Jesus taught in the synagogue, performed exorcisms, cured Simon Peter's mother-in-law, and then spent the entire evening healing the sick. "The whole city was gathered together about the door" (Mark 1:33) — pushing to get up close, hoping desperately for a miracle. How does Jesus heal each one? Does he look into their eyes with love and compassion, gently touching their faces? What does this mean to me, today? Do I eagerly seek out Christ's healing touch, the graces he wishes to shower on me — through the Eucharist and Reconciliation? How can I follow him more closely?

CHAPTER 7

Listening to Accompany

What does one do when he must talk a dangerous, possibly suicidal person out of unloading his AK-47 assault rifle while barricaded inside an apartment complex?

The first — and most important — step is to listen.

The FBI developed the Behavioral Change Stairway Model for dealing with these situations. It has five steps: active listening, empathy, rapport, influence, and behavioral change. But the most important step is the first one — a step back, a pause: *active listening*. The goal is to have the individual change his mind, and to change the outcome. But that is preceded by listening, empathy, and rapport.

The same can be said of any number of situations in which we find ourselves every day. We might need to ask our boss for a raise. Or we may seek to change the hearts and minds of those contemplating abortion or to bring an inactive Catholic back to the Church. Or we may hope to convince a relative to change destructive behavior to something positive. Or we want to convince our son home from college to get a summer job, *stat!*

All of these situations require motivating to action. The least likely way to get the college student bent on summer relaxation to start hustling for a job is to preach, nag, yell, or sanctimoniously describe your many summer jobs forty years ago. The worst way to convince your boss to give you a raise is to surprise him in the elevator and pressure him to make a decision by the time the doors open on the seventh floor. Your friend who has been away from the Church is not likely to take kindly to your exhortation that the wages of sin is death.

Though we think we shouldn't have to, the best way to motivate a son to find work is first to listen. Take the time to sit down with him over a soda and chat about his past year. Congratulate him for having finished the school year. Acknowledge his looking forward to reconnecting with old friends and his anxieties or uncertainties about how to navigate the job search. This is the encounter that Pope Francis talks about. Even if your son does not comply, the relationship (the bridge) remains intact.

Many times in life we must commit to listening even when it is hard — when we do not hear what we want to hear. Sometimes God is asking us to make a change we don't want to make. Sometimes our wife, children, friends, or colleagues do not tell us what we want to hear. We ask for music, but we hear static. Yet love is expressed in listening to the truth. We show our love for God by listening to his silence or by obeying his tough command. We show love to others by hearing them out even when we disagree or are disappointed.

We like to say: Keep the drawbridge down between you and God, and you and your neighbor. Let the conversation and dialogue continue on the bridge even if you don't like the message. Listen with respect and empathy, allowing love to be carried across the bridge.

Listening to Change

In his position as president of Catholic Charities, Art oversees a staff and more than 2,500 volunteers who generously serve the poor and needy in the many Catholic Charities programs — whether it is serving dinner at the homeless shelter, visiting prisoners, stocking the food pantry, or teaching immigrants and refugees how to speak English. Recently, one man volunteered to teach English as a second language to the large Hispanic population in a local town. He had previously expressed strong opinions on the fact that undocumented immigrants were "breaking the law" and shouldn't be here. However, after volunteering for several months, his heart was changed. He listened to their stories, he saw how dedicated they were to improving their language skills, and he noted how they often came to class after working two jobs. "They don't even go home until they have completed their homework," he told Art, amazed at the perseverance and commitment of these hardworking immigrants.

Because he listened and took the time to accompany these people, his heart was changed.

Pope Francis connects the dots for us when he talks about the Blessed Mother's listening and responsiveness in action. Mary attends carefully and responds immediately to serve her cousin Elizabeth when the angel Gabriel tells her that she will have a child and that her cousin is expecting. Having visited the Holy Land, we were struck by the distance that Mary traveled, all the way from Nazareth to her cousin's home in Ein Karem, in the hill country of Judea. It probably took several days of intense, possibly even dangerous travel. Yet Mary unhesitatingly undertook the trip. One of the aspects of the virtue of charity is that it should be *prompt*. Mary, exemplifying the virtue of charity, listened and responded promptly.

When Pope Francis visited Cuba in September 2015, he gave a homily at the National Shrine of the Virgen de la Caridad del Cobre, in which he invited all to a culture of encounter: "We are visited so that we can visit others; we are encountered so as to encounter others, we are loved so we can return that love."[1] Like Mary, we listen in order to accompany our neighbors in joyful times or in sorrow, building bridges and sowing seeds of reconciliation.

Pope Francis practices what he preaches. Whether making surprise visits to Muslim refugees, to a Roman shantytown, or to a nursing home; or taking selfies with young people or washing the feet of prisoners on Holy Thursday, Pope Francis literally takes it to the streets.

The Church as Field Hospital

One of Pope Francis' most vivid metaphors is that of the Church as field hospital:

> I like to use the image of a field hospital to describe this "Church that goes forth"; it exists where there is combat, it is not a solid structure with all the equipment where people go to receive treatment for both small and large infirmities. It is a mobile structure that offers first aid and immediate care, so that its soldiers do not die. It's a place for urgent care, not a place to see a specialist. I hope that the Jubilee will serve to reveal the Church's deeply maternal and merciful side, a Church that goes forth toward those who are "wounded," who are in need of an attentive ear, understanding, forgiveness, and love.[2]

We live five minutes away from the historic Manassas National Battlefield Park, where the bloody battles were fought in the backyards of Virginia farmers. The First Battle of Bull Run was a surprise to many of the local families. They were simple farmers, supporting their families and mostly just minding their own business. Suddenly they found themselves in the middle of the first major land battle of the Civil War. More than 4,800 men died — again, a surprise to many, considering congressmen and other civilians traveled from Washington to watch what they presumed to be a small skirmish.

The last thing these local farming families expected was to see bullets flying past their windows and to have to care for wounded soldiers in their living rooms.

But like the innkeeper of the Good Samaritan parable (Luke 10:25–37), they took people in. Their homes were transformed into field hospitals, set up near the combat zone to provide emergency care for the wounded.

Pope Francis calls us to rethink the way we approach our Catholic Faith. Are we called simply to work on our own spiritual progress, as we pray in solitary and comfortable silence in the cool, candle-lit church? Meanwhile, our Christian brothers and sisters are literally being martyred in other parts of the world. And our homeless and hungry brothers and sisters are wasting away in our streets for lack of both spiritual and physical resources. Pope Francis wants to banish the smug, comfortable, fortress-like view of our religion and faith. Instead, he wants us to go out, even into the margins:

> What should we do for the homeless man camped in front of our home, for the poor man who has nothing to eat, for the neighboring family who cannot make it to the end of the month due to the recession, because the husband lost his job? How should we behave with the immigrants who have survived the crossing and who land on our shores? What should we do for the elderly who are alone, abandoned, and who have no one?

... Reach out, know how to listen, advise them, and teach them through our own experience. By welcoming a marginalized person whose body is wounded and by welcoming the sinner whose soul is wounded, we put our credibility as Christians on the line. Let us always remember the words of Saint John of the Cross: "In the evening of life, we will be judged on love alone."[3]

Taking our "marching orders" from Pope Francis, we should practice our apostolate of the ear. We must put our listening skills to good use — first within our own families and then in our communities.

Pope Francis also speaks about "accompaniment" — that we should accompany those whom we would like to bring closer to Christ. Today, he says, we need to be people who accompany our brothers and sisters, walking with them rather than condemning them from a distance, practicing the art of listening. "Listening helps us to find the right gesture and word which shows that we are more than simply bystanders."[4]

Accompaniment has a very rich meaning. In simple terms, it means to meet people where they are and to treat them with the respect and the dignity they deserve as a child of God. Look for the best in them. As Father Robert Spitzer says, look for the Good News, not the bad news,[5] with our hearts open to seeing the other in a compassionate light. View their faults with patience (things take time!) "without making judgments about their responsibility and culpability (cf. Mt 7:1; Lk 6:37)."[6] Yet this is no mere exercise in tolerance or secular therapy; rather, we must always do it in light of our baptismal promises as Christians — to bring others closer to the Father. The central message of the Gospel is to bring everyone into relationship with the saving power of Christ under the merciful gaze of the Father. Everyone is in need of mercy and healing.

In his clinical practice, Art saw many men dragged into therapy because they had been caught by their wife watching pornography or engaging in other sexual mischief. This was intensely humiliating for both husband and wife, and it took great humility to visit a therapist. Often the wife would not want to be in therapy since "it is his problem." Art would agree that it is his problem and his responsibility to change. But he would invite the spouse to be a part of the healing process — and not a part of the humiliating or blaming process. "He will need your help to turn his life around," Art would say. "So let me start working with him, but soon we will invite you in, because all major changes in his life must involve you, his beloved wife." This was an invitation to accompany and to promote healing through the unity and love of marriage.

God himself accompanies each of us on our unique journey. He sent his only Son to become man, so that he could accompany us. "For our sake he made him to be sin who knew no sin, so that in him we might become the righteousness of God" (2 Corinthians 5:21). He himself accompanies us, so that we might also become one with him.

— PRACTICAL APPLICATION —

Try this exercise that Pope Francis recommends. Instead of tossing a coin to a needy person, walk over and place it in his or her hand, look them in the eyes, and ask their name and how they are doing. Listen to them without feeling the need to solve their problems. Just listen with empathy, promise to pray for them, and ask for their prayers, too. This is mercy, a gift from God, the "ultimate and supreme act by which God comes to meet us. Mercy: the fundamental law that dwells in the heart of every person who looks sincerely into the eyes of his brothers and sisters on the path of life."[7]

NOTES

Chapter 1: Listening: The Most Important Thing

[1] Pope Benedict XVI, Angelus address (October 4, 2009).

[2] Pope Francis, quoted in *America* (October 17, 2015), http://www.americamagazine.org/content/dispatches/pope-francis-reminds-synod-he-has-last-word (accessed August 8, 2017).

[3] Pope Benedict XVI, *Light of the World: The Pope, the Church, and the Signs of the Times: A Conversation with Peter Seewald*, trans. Michael J. Miller and Adrian J. Walker (San Francisco: Ignatius Press, 2010), p. 62.

[4] Pope Benedict XVI, *The Nature and Mission of Theology: Essays to Orient Theology in Today's Debates*, trans. Adrian Walker (San Francisco: Ignatius Press, 2011), p. 33.

[5] Pope Francis, Address on the 48th World Communications Day (June 1, 2014).

[6] Pope Francis, *Evangelii Gaudium* (on the proclamation of the Gospel in today's world), 169.

[7] Pope Benedict XVI, *The Blessing of Christmas: Meditations for the Season* (San Francisco: Ignatius Press, 2007), p. 90.

Chapter 2: Listening to Others

[1] Pope Francis (2016-01-12), *The Name of God Is Mercy* (Kindle locations 275-276). Random House Publishing Group. Kindle Edition.

[2] Sherry A. Weddell, *Forming Intentional Disciples: The Path to Knowing and Following Jesus* (Huntington, IN: Our Sunday Visitor, 2012), p.145.

[3] Pope Francis, *Evangelii Gaudium*, 46.

[4] Pope Francis, *Amoris Laetitia* (on love in the family), 137.

[5] Pope Francis, *Evangelii Gaudium*, 169.

[6] Adam S. McHugh, *The Listening Life: Embracing Attentiveness in a World of Distraction* (Downers Grove, IL: InterVarsity Press Books, 2015), pp. 81–82.

[7] Henri J. M. Nouwen, *Here and Now: Living in the Spirit* (New York: Crossroad Publishing, 1994), p. 140.

[8] Pope Francis, *Amoris Laetitia*, 97.

9 University of Georgia, "Poverty simulation helps students develop empathy," *Columns* (April 18, 2011), http://columns.uga.edu/news /article/poverty-simulation-helps-students/ (accessed August 8, 2017).

Chapter 3: Listening to Your Heart

1 Elizabeth Wagner, *Seasons in My Garden: Meditations from a Hermitage* (Notre Dame, IN: Ave Maria Press, 2016), p. 93.
2 Ibid., p. 95.
3 Mother Dolores Hart, O.S.B., and Richard DeNeut (2013-05-07), *The Ear of the Heart: An Actress' Journey from Hollywood to Holy Vows* (Kindle locations 2770-2771). Ignatius Press. Kindle Edition.
4 Ibid. (Kindle locations 3032-3034).
5 Dietrich Von Hildebrand, *The Heart: Source of Christian Affectivity* (Chicago: Franciscan Herald Press, 1977), p. 112.
6 St. Teresa of Ávila, *Interior Castle*, trans. Allison Peers (New York: Doubleday, 1989), p. 38.
7 John M. Gottman, Ph.D., and Julie Schwartz Gottman, Ph.D., *Ten Lessons to Transform Your Marriage: America's Love Lab Experts Share Their Strategies for Strengthening Your Relationship* (New York: Crown Publishers, 2006), p. 131.
8 Ibid., p. 145.

Chapter 4: Listening to Criticism

1 Gottman, *Ten Lessons to Transform Your Marriage*, p. 25.
2 Art and Laraine Bennett, *The Temperament God Gave Your Spouse* (Manchester, NH: Sophia Institute Press, 2008).
3 Aldophe Tanquerey, S.S., D.D., *The Spiritual Life: A Treatise on Ascetical and Mystical Theology* (Rockford, IL: Tan Books, 2000; originally published in 1930), p. 222.
4 John Gottman, Ph.D., *Why Marriages Succeed or Fail: And How You Can Make Yours Last* (New York: Fireside Books, 1994), p. 110.
5 Thomas Merton, *New Seeds of Contemplation* (New York: New Directions, Inc., 1972, 2007), p. 34.
6 Joseph Cardinal Ratzinger, *Introduction to Christianity, Second Edition* (San Francisco: Ignatius Press, 2004), p. 301.

Chapter 5: Listening to Wisdom

[1] Judith Valente, *Atchison Blue: A Search for Silence, a Spiritual Home, and a Living Faith* (Notre Dame, IN: Sorin Books, 2013), p. 20.

[2] Thomas Merton, *The Wisdom of the Desert* (New York: New Directions, 1970), p. 52.

[3] Ibid., p. 63.

[4] *The Liturgy of the Hours*, Vol. III (New York: Catholic Book Publishing, 1975), p. 282.

[5] Ibid.

[6] John A. Hardon, S.J., "A Eucharistic Retreat: Meditation #12," from the Archives of Father John A. Hardon, S.J., http://www .therealpresence.org/archives/Eucharist/Eucharist_050.htm (accessed August 8, 2017).

[7] Pope Francis, "The Spirit of Wisdom Triumphs Over Worldly Curiosity," *L'Osservatore Romano*, English edition (November 22, 2013), n. 47.

[8] Ibid.

[9] John Hardon, S.J., "Pentecost: The Happiness of the Possession of the Truth," Fr. John A. Hardon, S.J. Archive and Guild, http://www .hardonsj.org/pentecost-the-happiness-of-possession-of-the-truth (accessed August 8, 2017). Copyright © 1998 Inter Mirifica.

[10] *The Liturgy of the Hours*, Vol. III, pp. 246, 247.

[11] Patrick Henry Reardon, "Abigail & the Way of Wisdom," *Touchstone* (Spring 1996), http://www.touchstonemag.com/archives/article .php?id=09-02-026-f (accessed August 8, 2017).

Chapter 6: Listening to God

[1] Eucharistic Prayer I, *The Roman Missal*.

[2] *The Liturgy of the Hours*, Book IV (New York: Catholic Book Publishing Co., 1975), p. 231.

[3] Joseph Ratzinger, *The Blessing of Christmas* (San Francisco: Ignatius Press, 2007), p. 92.

[4] McHugh, *The Listening Life*, p. 66.

[5] Joseph Cardinal Ratzinger, *Co-Workers of the Truth: Meditations for Every Day of the Year* (San Francisco: Ignatius Press, 1992), p. 240.

[6] All details have been changed to protect the families involved.

Notes

7 Sarah Salviander, blog post, https://sixdayscience.com/2015/05/11
/my-testimony/ (accessed August 23, 2017).

8 Ratzinger, *Co-Workers of the Truth*, p. 338.

9 Fr. Kilian J. Healy, *Awakening Your Soul to the Presence of God*
(Manchester, NH: Sophia Institute Press, 1999; originally published in
New York by the Declan X. McMullen Co., Inc.,1948), p. 39.

10 Pope Francis, Angelus Address, July 17, 2016.

11 Father Jacques Philippe, *Searching for and Maintaining Peace: A Small
Treatise on Peace of Heart* (New York: Alba House, 2002), p. 72.

12 Brian Kolodiejchuk, M.C., ed., *Mother Teresa: Come Be My Light: The
Private Writings of the Saint of Calcutta* (New York: Doubleday, 2010),
p. 210.

13 Eugene Boylan, *Difficulties in Mental Prayer* (Princeton, NJ: Scepter
Press, 1997), p. 141.

14 Erasmo Leiva-Merikakis, *Fire of Mercy, Heart of the Word: Meditations
on the Gospel according to Saint Matthew*, Vol. 3. (San Francisco: Ignatius
Press, 2012), p. 468.

15 Ibid., p. 469.

Chapter 7: Listening to Accompany

1 Radiovaticana.va 22/09/2015: "Pope Francis: follow Mary on the path
to visitation," http://en.radiovaticana.va/news/2015/09/22/pope_
francis_follow_mary_on_the_path_to_visitation/1173858 (accessed
August 8, 2017).

2 Pope Francis (2016-01-12), *The Name of God Is Mercy* (Kindle
locations 499-504). Random House Publishing Group. Kindle Edition.

3 Ibid. (Kindle locations 819-822).

4 Pope Francis, *Evangelii Gaudium*, 171.

5 Robert Spitzer, S.J., *The Spirit of Leadership* audio CD (Ann Arbor, MI:
Spitzer Center for Ethical Leadership, 2006).

6 Pope Francis, *Evangelii Gaudium*, 172.

7 Pope Francis (2016-01-12), *The Name of God Is Mercy* (Kindle
locations 845-846).

Also by the Bennetts

THE TEMPERAMENT GOD GAVE YOUR KIDS
By Art and Laraine Bennett
Understanding a child's unique temperament is key to effective discipline and a strategy for nurturing a child's strengths. Using classical wisdom, modern counseling science, Catholic spirituality, and wonderful storytelling, Art and Laraine Bennett help parents become active, compassionate participants in their child's social and spiritual formation, bringing peace, happiness, and holiness to the entire family.
Inventory No. T1244

A YEAR OF GRACE: 365 REFLECTIONS FOR CAREGIVERS
By Laraine Bennett
Here is a daily respite for the weary caregiver, a chance to recharge and refresh the mind and spirit, and to look anew, with gratitude and hope, at the value of every human life.
Inventory No. T1436

TO ORDER FROM OUR SUNDAY VISITOR
Call: 800-348-2440
Fax: 800-498-6709
Online: OSV.com